Remembering the City that Never Sleeps!

Travel Journal

NYC Edition

Activinotes

Activinotes

DAILY JOURNALS, PLANNERS, NOTEBOOKS AND OTHER BLANK BOOKS

Travel Journal

Date _____

_____
Place to Explore

i ♥ NYC

Things to See & Do :

- ☐ ....
- ☐ ....
- ☐ ....
- ☐ ....
- ☐ ....
- ☐ ....
- ☐ ....
- ☐ ....
- ☐ ....

Things to Observe :

- ☐ _____
- ☐ _____
- ☐ _____
- ☐ _____
- ☐ _____
- ☐ _____
- ☐ _____

Adventure to Have :

- ☐ _____
- ☐ _____
- ☐ _____
- ☐ _____
- ☐ _____
- ☐ _____
- ☐ _____

Places to Mingle :

- ☐ _____
- ☐ _____
- ☐ _____
- ☐ _____
- ☐ _____
- ☐ _____
- ☐ _____

Travel Journal

Sreets to Check Out :

☐ _____
☐ _____
☐ _____
☐ _____
☐ _____
☐ _____
☐ _____

People to Meet :

☐ _____
☐ _____
☐ _____
☐ _____
☐ _____
☐ _____
☐ _____

Shops to Visit :

☐ _____
☐ _____
☐ _____
☐ _____
☐ _____
☐ _____
☐ _____

place your photo here

Travel Journal

i ♥ NYC

Date _____

_____
Place to Explore

Things to See & Do :

☐ ....
☐ ....
☐ ....
☐ ....
☐ ....
☐ ....
☐ ....
☐ ....
☐ ....
☐ ....

Things to Observe :

☐ _____
☐ _____
☐ _____
☐ _____
☐ _____
☐ _____
☐ _____

Places to Mingle :

☐ _____
☐ _____
☐ _____
☐ _____
☐ _____
☐ _____
☐ _____

Adventure to Have :

☐ _____
☐ _____
☐ _____
☐ _____
☐ _____
☐ _____

Travel Journal

Sreets to Check Out :

- ☐ _____
- ☐ _____
- ☐ _____
- ☐ _____
- ☐ _____
- ☐ _____
- ☐ _____

People to Meet :

- ☐ _____
- ☐ _____
- ☐ _____
- ☐ _____
- ☐ _____
- ☐ _____
- ☐ _____

Shops to Visit :

- ☐ _____
- ☐ _____
- ☐ _____
- ☐ _____
- ☐ _____
- ☐ _____
- ☐ _____

place your photo here

Travel Journal

i
♥
NYC

Date _____

_____
Place to Explore

Things to See & Do :

- ☐ ....
- ☐ ....
- ☐ ....
- ☐ ....
- ☐ ....
- ☐ ....
- ☐ ....
- ☐ ....
- ☐ ....

Things to Observe :

- ☐ _____
- ☐ _____
- ☐ _____
- ☐ _____
- ☐ _____
- ☐ _____
- ☐ _____

Places to Mingle : 🍴♡🍴

- ☐ _____
- ☐ _____
- ☐ _____
- ☐ _____
- ☐ _____
- ☐ _____
- ☐ _____

Adventure to Have :

- ☐ _____
- ☐ _____
- ☐ _____
- ☐ _____
- ☐ _____
- ☐ _____
- ☐ _____

Travel Journal

I ♥ NYC

Sreets to Check Out :

- ☐ _____
- ☐ _____
- ☐ _____
- ☐ _____
- ☐ _____
- ☐ _____
- ☐ _____

People to Meet :

- ☐ _____
- ☐ _____
- ☐ _____
- ☐ _____
- ☐ _____
- ☐ _____
- ☐ _____

Shops to Visit :

- ☐ _____
- ☐ _____
- ☐ _____
- ☐ _____
- ☐ _____
- ☐ _____
- ☐ _____

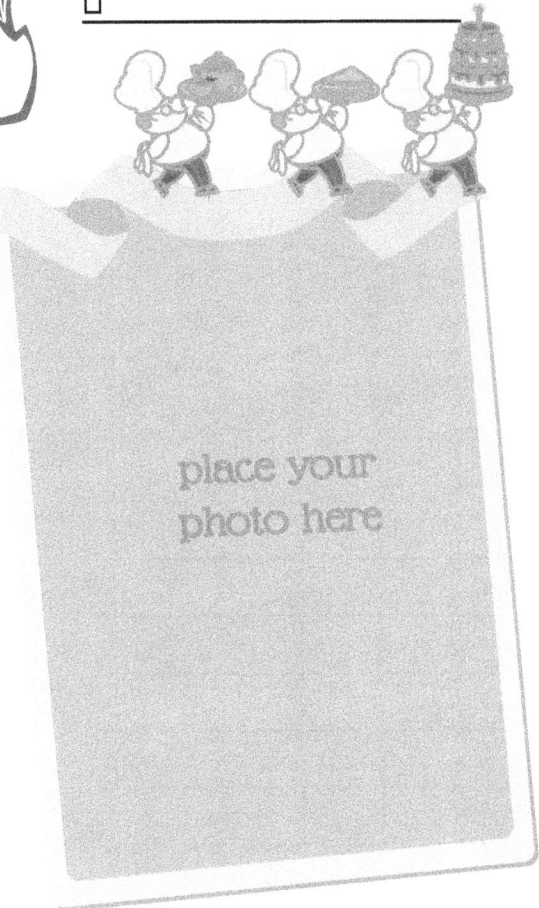

place your
photo here

Travel Journal

Date _____

<u>_____</u>
Place to Explore

i
♥
NYC

Things to See & Do :

- ☐ ....
- ☐ ....
- ☐ ....
- ☐ ....
- ☐ ....
- ☐ ....
- ☐ ....
- ☐ ....
- ☐ ....
- ☐ ....

Things to Observe :

- ☐ _____
- ☐ _____
- ☐ _____
- ☐ _____
- ☐ _____
- ☐ _____
- ☐ _____

Places to Mingle :

- ☐ _____
- ☐ _____
- ☐ _____
- ☐ _____
- ☐ _____
- ☐ _____
- ☐ _____

Adventure to Have :

- ☐ _____
- ☐ _____
- ☐ _____
- ☐ _____
- ☐ _____
- ☐ _____
- ☐ _____

Travel Journal

I ♥ NYC

Sreets to Check Out :

- ☐ _____
- ☐ _____
- ☐ _____
- ☐ _____
- ☐ _____
- ☐ _____
- ☐ _____

People to Meet :

- ☐ _____
- ☐ _____
- ☐ _____
- ☐ _____
- ☐ _____
- ☐ _____
- ☐ _____

Shops to Visit :

- ☐ _____
- ☐ _____
- ☐ _____
- ☐ _____
- ☐ _____
- ☐ _____
- ☐ _____

place your photo here

Travel Journal

Date _____

_____
Place to Explore

i
♥
NYC

Things to See & Do :

- ☐ ....
- ☐ ....
- ☐ ....
- ☐ ....
- ☐ ....
- ☐ ....
- ☐ ....
- ☐ ....
- ☐ ....
- ☐ ....

Things to Observe :

- ☐ _____
- ☐ _____
- ☐ _____
- ☐ _____
- ☐ _____
- ☐ _____
- ☐ _____

Places to Mingle :

- ☐ _____
- ☐ _____
- ☐ _____
- ☐ _____
- ☐ _____
- ☐ _____
- ☐ _____

Adventure to Have :

- ☐ _____
- ☐ _____
- ☐ _____
- ☐ _____
- ☐ _____
- ☐ _____
- ☐ _____

Travel Journal

i ♥ NYC

Sreets to Check Out :

- ☐ _____
- ☐ _____
- ☐ _____
- ☐ _____
- ☐ _____
- ☐ _____
- ☐ _____

People to Meet :

- ☐ _____
- ☐ _____
- ☐ _____
- ☐ _____
- ☐ _____
- ☐ _____
- ☐ _____

Shops to Visit :

- ☐ _____
- ☐ _____
- ☐ _____
- ☐ _____
- ☐ _____
- ☐ _____
- ☐ _____

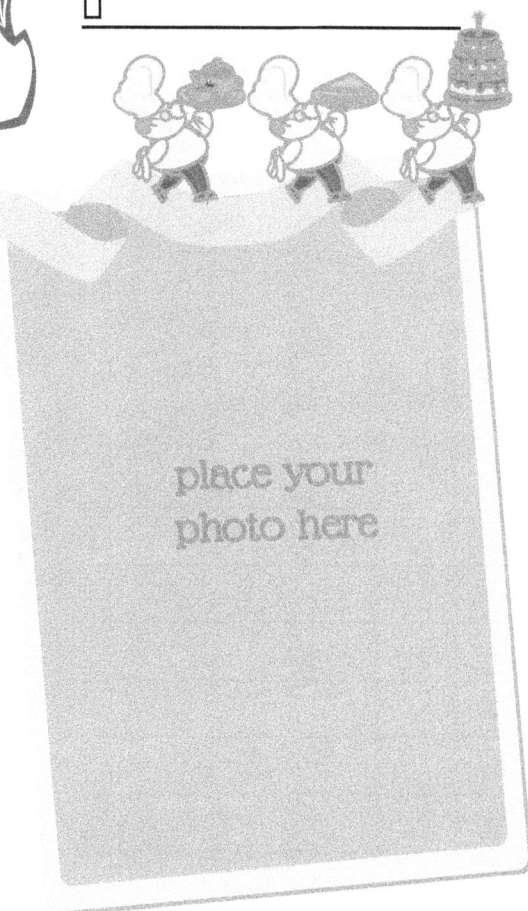

place your photo here

Travel Journal

Date _____

_____
Place to Explore

i ♥ NYC

Things to See & Do :

- ☐ ....
- ☐ ....
- ☐ ....
- ☐ ....
- ☐ ....
- ☐ ....
- ☐ ....
- ☐ ....
- ☐ ....

Things to Observe :

- ☐ _____
- ☐ _____
- ☐ _____
- ☐ _____
- ☐ _____
- ☐ _____
- ☐ _____

Places to Mingle :

- ☐ _____
- ☐ _____
- ☐ _____
- ☐ _____
- ☐ _____
- ☐ _____
- ☐ _____

Adventure to Have :

- ☐ _____
- ☐ _____
- ☐ _____
- ☐ _____
- ☐ _____
- ☐ _____
- ☐ _____

Travel Journal

i ♥ NYC

Sreets to Check Out :

- ☐ _____
- ☐ _____
- ☐ _____
- ☐ _____
- ☐ _____
- ☐ _____
- ☐ _____

People to Meet :

- ☐ _____
- ☐ _____
- ☐ _____
- ☐ _____
- ☐ _____
- ☐ _____
- ☐ _____

Shops to Visit :

- ☐ _____
- ☐ _____
- ☐ _____
- ☐ _____
- ☐ _____
- ☐ _____
- ☐ _____

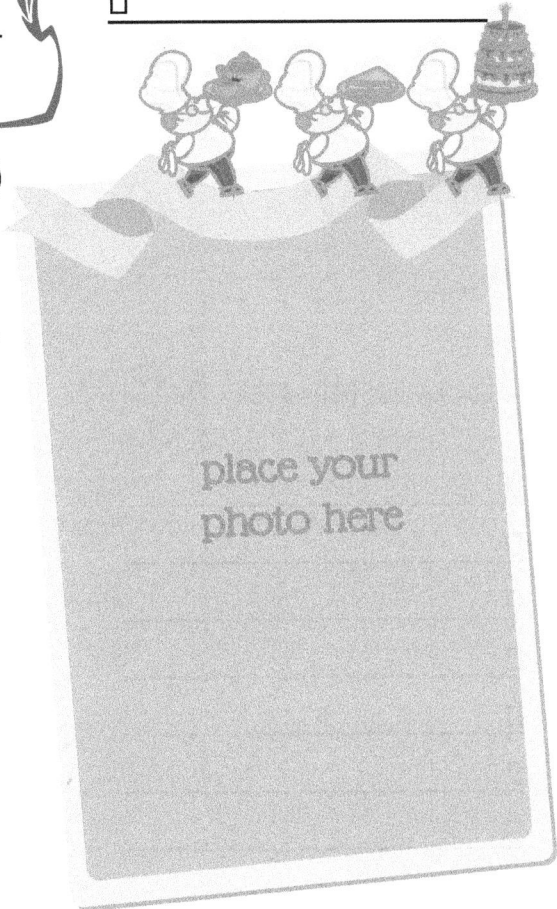

place your
photo here

Travel Journal

Date _____

_____
Place to Explore

i ♥ NYC

Things to See & Do :

- ☐ ....
- ☐ ....
- ☐ ....
- ☐ ....
- ☐ ....
- ☐ ....
- ☐ ....
- ☐ ....
- ☐ ....

Things to Observe :

- ☐ _____
- ☐ _____
- ☐ _____
- ☐ _____
- ☐ _____
- ☐ _____
- ☐ _____

Places to Mingle :

- ☐ _____
- ☐ _____
- ☐ _____
- ☐ _____
- ☐ _____
- ☐ _____
- ☐ _____

Adventure to Have :

- ☐ _____
- ☐ _____
- ☐ _____
- ☐ _____
- ☐ _____
- ☐ _____
- ☐ _____

Travel Journal

i ♥ NYC

Sreets to Check Out :

☐ _____
☐ _____
☐ _____
☐ _____
☐ _____
☐ _____
☐ _____

People to Meet :

☐ _____
☐ _____
☐ _____
☐ _____
☐ _____
☐ _____
☐ _____

Shops to Visit :

☐ _____
☐ _____
☐ _____
☐ _____
☐ _____
☐ _____
☐ _____

place your photo here

Travel Journal

i ♥ NYC

Date _____

_____
Place to Explore

Things to See & Do :

- ☐ ....
- ☐ ....
- ☐ ....
- ☐ ....
- ☐ ....
- ☐ ....
- ☐ ....
- ☐ ....
- ☐ ....

Things to Observe :

- ☐ _____
- ☐ _____
- ☐ _____
- ☐ _____
- ☐ _____
- ☐ _____
- ☐ _____

Places to Mingle :

- ☐ _____
- ☐ _____
- ☐ _____
- ☐ _____
- ☐ _____
- ☐ _____
- ☐ _____

Adventure to Have :

- ☐ _____
- ☐ _____
- ☐ _____
- ☐ _____
- ☐ _____
- ☐ _____

Travel Journal

i ♥ NYC

Sreets to Check Out :

- ☐ _____
- ☐ _____
- ☐ _____
- ☐ _____
- ☐ _____
- ☐ _____
- ☐ _____

People to Meet :

- ☐ _____
- ☐ _____
- ☐ _____
- ☐ _____
- ☐ _____
- ☐ _____
- ☐ _____

Shops to Visit :

- ☐ _____
- ☐ _____
- ☐ _____
- ☐ _____
- ☐ _____
- ☐ _____
- ☐ _____

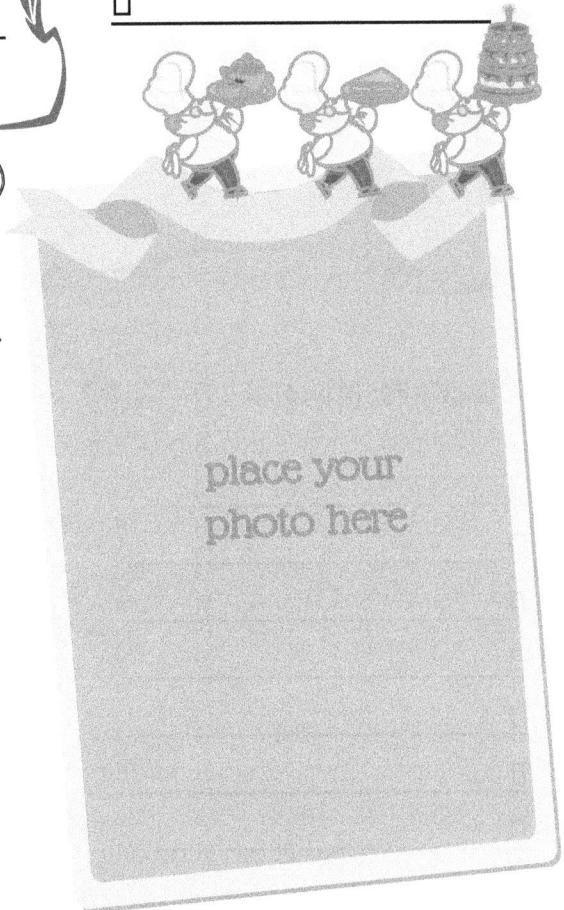

place your photo here

Travel Journal

Date _____

_____
Place to Explore

i
♥
NYC

Things to See & Do :

- ☐ ....
- ☐ ....
- ☐ ....
- ☐ ....
- ☐ ....
- ☐ ....
- ☐ ....
- ☐ ....
- ☐ ....

Things to Observe :

- ☐ _____
- ☐ _____
- ☐ _____
- ☐ _____
- ☐ _____
- ☐ _____
- ☐ _____

Places to Mingle : 🍴♥🥄

- ☐ _____
- ☐ _____
- ☐ _____
- ☐ _____
- ☐ _____
- ☐ _____
- ☐ _____

Adventure to Have :

- ☐ _____
- ☐ _____
- ☐ _____
- ☐ _____
- ☐ _____
- ☐ _____

Travel Journal

Sreets to Check Out :

- ☐ _____
- ☐ _____
- ☐ _____
- ☐ _____
- ☐ _____
- ☐ _____
- ☐ _____

People to Meet :

- ☐ _____
- ☐ _____
- ☐ _____
- ☐ _____
- ☐ _____
- ☐ _____
- ☐ _____

Shops to Visit :

- ☐ _____
- ☐ _____
- ☐ _____
- ☐ _____
- ☐ _____
- ☐ _____
- ☐ _____

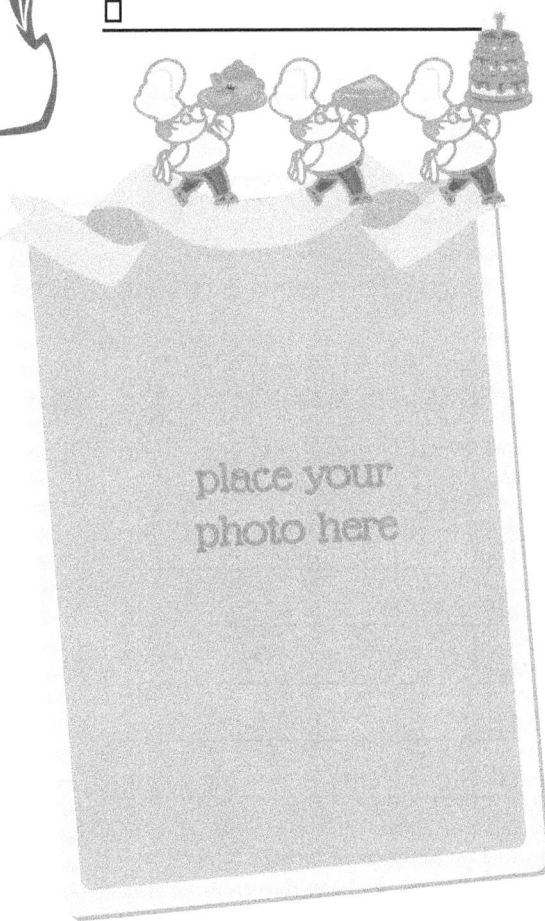

place your
photo here

Travel Journal

i ♥ NYC

Date _____

_____
Place to Explore

Things to See & Do :

☐ ....
☐ ....
☐ ....
☐ ....
☐ ....
☐ ....
☐ ....
☐ ....
☐ ....

Things to Observe :

☐ _____
☐ _____
☐ _____
☐ _____
☐ _____
☐ _____
☐ _____

Places to Mingle :

☐ _____
☐ _____
☐ _____
☐ _____
☐ _____
☐ _____
☐ _____

Adventure to Have :

☐ _____
☐ _____
☐ _____
☐ _____
☐ _____
☐ _____

Travel Journal

i ♥ NYC

Sreets to Check Out :

☐ _____
☐ _____
☐ _____
☐ _____
☐ _____
☐ _____
☐ _____

People to Meet :

☐ _____
☐ _____
☐ _____
☐ _____
☐ _____
☐ _____
☐ _____

Shops to Visit :

☐ _____
☐ _____
☐ _____
☐ _____
☐ _____
☐ _____
☐ _____

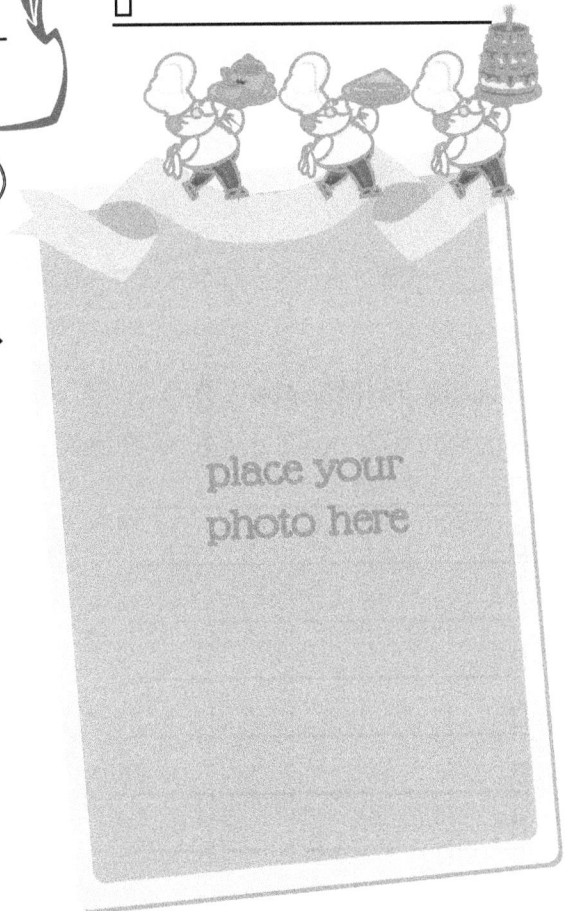

place your photo here

Travel Journal

i ♥ NYC

Date _____

Place to Explore

Things to See & Do :

- ☐ ....
- ☐ ....
- ☐ ....
- ☐ ....
- ☐ ....
- ☐ ....
- ☐ ....
- ☐ ....
- ☐ ....
- ☐ ....

Things to Observe :

- ☐ _____
- ☐ _____
- ☐ _____
- ☐ _____
- ☐ _____
- ☐ _____
- ☐ _____

Places to Mingle : 🍴♡🍴

- ☐ _____
- ☐ _____
- ☐ _____
- ☐ _____
- ☐ _____
- ☐ _____
- ☐ _____

Adventure to Have :

- ☐ _____
- ☐ _____
- ☐ _____
- ☐ _____
- ☐ _____
- ☐ _____
- ☐ _____

Travel Journal

i ❤ NYC

Sreets to Check Out :

- ☐ _____
- ☐ _____
- ☐ _____
- ☐ _____
- ☐ _____
- ☐ _____
- ☐ _____

People to Meet :

- ☐ _____
- ☐ _____
- ☐ _____
- ☐ _____
- ☐ _____
- ☐ _____
- ☐ _____

Shops to Visit :

- ☐ _____
- ☐ _____
- ☐ _____
- ☐ _____
- ☐ _____
- ☐ _____
- ☐ _____

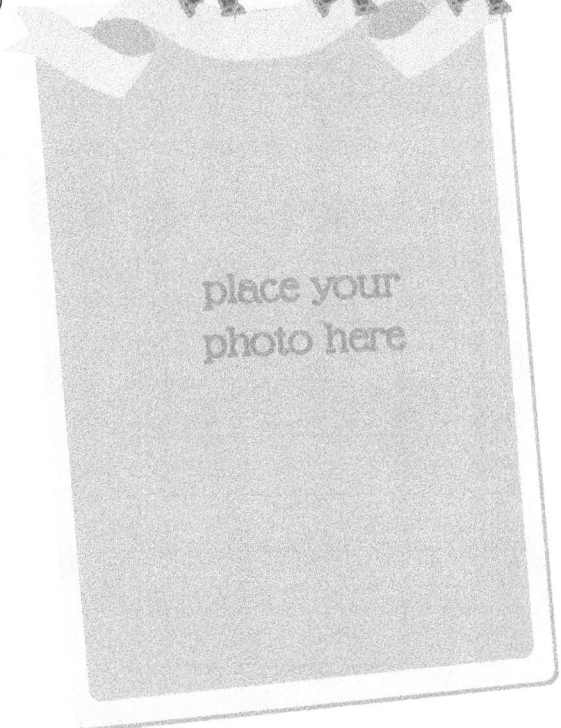

place your photo here

Travel Journal

Date _____

_____
Place to Explore

i
♥
NYC

Things to See & Do :

- ☐ ....
- ☐ ....
- ☐ ....
- ☐ ....
- ☐ ....
- ☐ ....
- ☐ ....
- ☐ ....
- ☐ ....

Things to Observe :

- ☐ _____
- ☐ _____
- ☐ _____
- ☐ _____
- ☐ _____
- ☐ _____
- ☐ _____

Places to Mingle : 🍴♡🥄

- ☐ _____
- ☐ _____
- ☐ _____
- ☐ _____
- ☐ _____
- ☐ _____
- ☐ _____

Adventure to Have :

- ☐ _____
- ☐ _____
- ☐ _____
- ☐ _____
- ☐ _____
- ☐ _____
- ☐ _____

Travel Journal

i ♥ NYC

Sreets to Check Out :

- ☐ _____
- ☐ _____
- ☐ _____
- ☐ _____
- ☐ _____
- ☐ _____
- ☐ _____

People to Meet :

- ☐ _____
- ☐ _____
- ☐ _____
- ☐ _____
- ☐ _____
- ☐ _____
- ☐ _____

Shops to Visit :

- ☐ _____
- ☐ _____
- ☐ _____
- ☐ _____
- ☐ _____
- ☐ _____
- ☐ _____

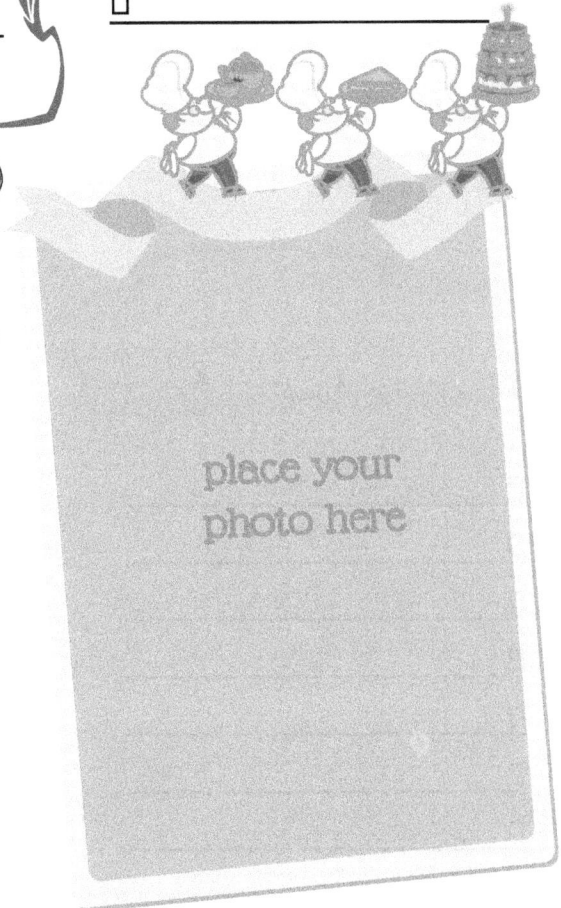

place your photo here

Travel Journal

i ♥ NYC

Date _____

_____
Place to Explore

Things to See & Do :

- ☐ ....
- ☐ ....
- ☐ ....
- ☐ ....
- ☐ ....
- ☐ ....
- ☐ ....
- ☐ ....
- ☐ ....

Things to Observe :

- ☐ _____
- ☐ _____
- ☐ _____
- ☐ _____
- ☐ _____
- ☐ _____
- ☐ _____

Places to Mingle :

- ☐ _____
- ☐ _____
- ☐ _____
- ☐ _____
- ☐ _____
- ☐ _____
- ☐ _____

Adventure to Have :

- ☐ _____
- ☐ _____
- ☐ _____
- ☐ _____
- ☐ _____
- ☐ _____
- ☐ _____

Travel Journal

i ♥ NYC

Sreets to Check Out :

- ☐ _____
- ☐ _____
- ☐ _____
- ☐ _____
- ☐ _____
- ☐ _____
- ☐ _____

People to Meet :

- ☐ _____
- ☐ _____
- ☐ _____
- ☐ _____
- ☐ _____
- ☐ _____
- ☐ _____

Shops to Visit :

- ☐ _____
- ☐ _____
- ☐ _____
- ☐ _____
- ☐ _____
- ☐ _____
- ☐ _____

place your photo here

Travel Journal

Date _____

_____
Place to Explore

i ♥ NYC

Things to See & Do :

- ☐ ....
- ☐ _____
- ☐ ....
- ☐ _____
- ☐ _____
- ☐ _____
- ☐ _____
- ☐ _____
- ☐ ....

Things to Observe :

- ☐ _____
- ☐ _____
- ☐ _____
- ☐ _____
- ☐ _____
- ☐ _____
- ☐ _____

Places to Mingle :

- ☐ _____
- ☐ _____
- ☐ _____
- ☐ _____
- ☐ _____
- ☐ _____
- ☐ _____

Adventure to Have :

- ☐ _____
- ☐ _____
- ☐ _____
- ☐ _____
- ☐ _____
- ☐ _____
- ☐ _____

Travel Journal

i ♥ NYC

Sreets to Check Out :

- ☐ _____
- ☐ _____
- ☐ _____
- ☐ _____
- ☐ _____
- ☐ _____
- ☐ _____

People to Meet :

- ☐ _____
- ☐ _____
- ☐ _____
- ☐ _____
- ☐ _____
- ☐ _____
- ☐ _____

Shops to Visit :

- ☐ _____
- ☐ _____
- ☐ _____
- ☐ _____
- ☐ _____
- ☐ _____
- ☐ _____

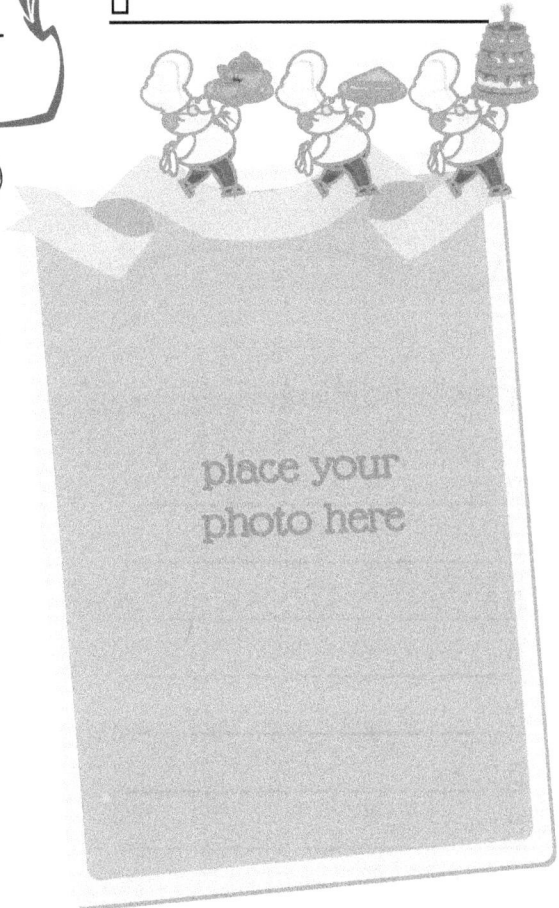
place your photo here

Travel Journal

i ♥ NYC

Date _____

_____
Place to Explore

Things to See & Do :

- ☐ ....
- ☐ ....
- ☐ ....
- ☐ ....
- ☐ ....
- ☐ ....
- ☐ ....
- ☐ ....
- ☐ ....
- ☐ ....

Things to Observe :

- ☐ _____
- ☐ _____
- ☐ _____
- ☐ _____
- ☐ _____
- ☐ _____
- ☐ _____

Places to Mingle : 🍴♥🍴

- ☐ _____
- ☐ _____
- ☐ _____
- ☐ _____
- ☐ _____
- ☐ _____
- ☐ _____

Adventure to Have :

- ☐ _____
- ☐ _____
- ☐ _____
- ☐ _____
- ☐ _____
- ☐ _____
- ☐ _____

Travel Journal

i ♥ NYC

Sreets to Check Out :

- ☐ _____
- ☐ _____
- ☐ _____
- ☐ _____
- ☐ _____
- ☐ _____
- ☐ _____

People to Meet :

- ☐ _____
- ☐ _____
- ☐ _____
- ☐ _____
- ☐ _____
- ☐ _____
- ☐ _____

Shops to Visit :

- ☐ _____
- ☐ _____
- ☐ _____
- ☐ _____
- ☐ _____
- ☐ _____
- ☐ _____

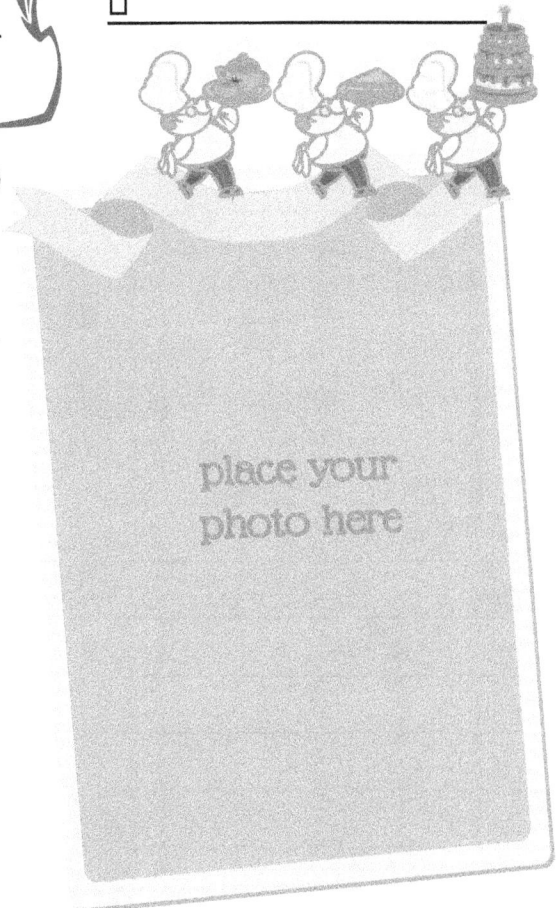

place your photo here

Travel Journal

i ♥ NYC

Date _____

_____
Place to Explore

Things to See & Do :

- ☐ ....
- ☐ ....
- ☐ ....
- ☐ ....
- ☐ ....
- ☐ ....
- ☐ ....
- ☐ ....
- ☐ ....

Things to Observe :

- ☐ _____
- ☐ _____
- ☐ _____
- ☐ _____
- ☐ _____
- ☐ _____
- ☐ _____

Places to Mingle :

- ☐ _____
- ☐ _____
- ☐ _____
- ☐ _____
- ☐ _____
- ☐ _____
- ☐ _____

Adventure to Have :

- ☐ _____
- ☐ _____
- ☐ _____
- ☐ _____
- ☐ _____
- ☐ _____
- ☐ _____

Travel Journal

i ♥ NYC

Sreets to Check Out :

- ☐ _____
- ☐ _____
- ☐ _____
- ☐ _____
- ☐ _____
- ☐ _____
- ☐ _____

People to Meet :

- ☐ _____
- ☐ _____
- ☐ _____
- ☐ _____
- ☐ _____
- ☐ _____
- ☐ _____

Shops to Visit :

- ☐ _____
- ☐ _____
- ☐ _____
- ☐ _____
- ☐ _____
- ☐ _____
- ☐ _____

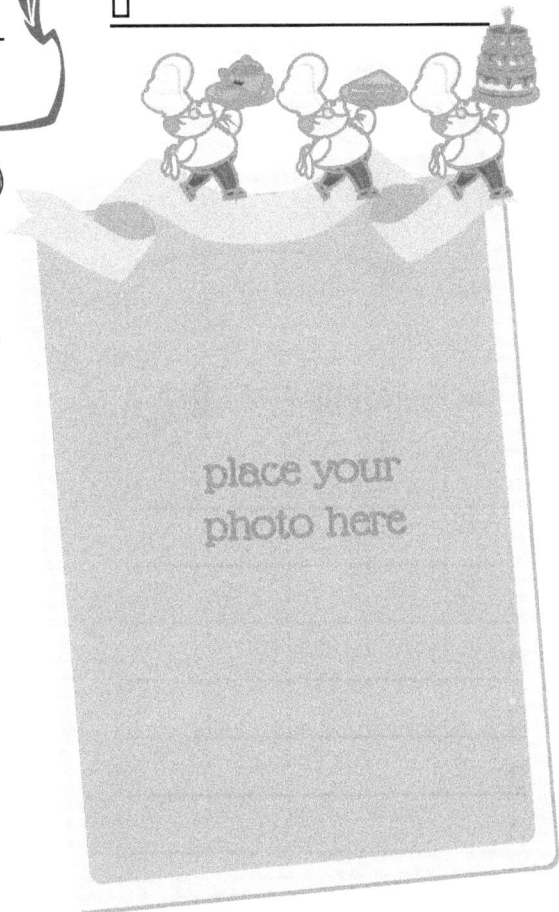

place your photo here

Travel Journal

Date _____

_____
Place to Explore

i
♥
NYC

Things to See & Do :

☐ ....
☐ ....
☐ ....
☐ ....
☐ ....
☐ ....
☐ ....
☐ ....
☐ ....
☐ ....

Things to Observe :

☐ _____
☐ _____
☐ _____
☐ _____
☐ _____
☐ _____
☐ _____

Places to Mingle :

☐ _____
☐ _____
☐ _____
☐ _____
☐ _____
☐ _____
☐ _____

Adventure to Have :

☐ _____
☐ _____
☐ _____
☐ _____
☐ _____
☐ _____
☐ _____

Travel Journal

i ♥ NYC

Sreets to Check Out :

- [ ] _____
- [ ] _____
- [ ] _____
- [ ] _____
- [ ] _____
- [ ] _____
- [ ] _____

People to Meet :

- [ ] _____
- [ ] _____
- [ ] _____
- [ ] _____
- [ ] _____
- [ ] _____
- [ ] _____

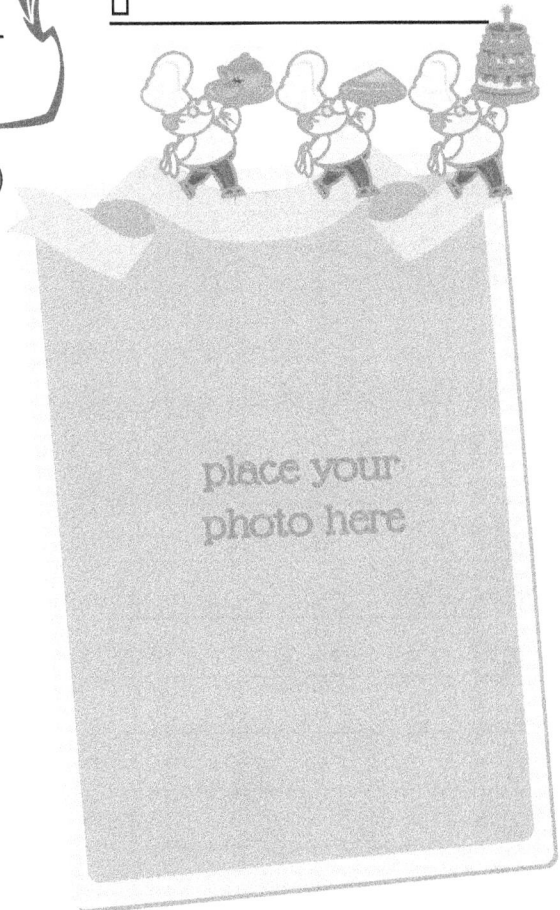

place your photo here

Shops to Visit :

- [ ] _____
- [ ] _____
- [ ] _____
- [ ] _____
- [ ] _____
- [ ] _____
- [ ] _____

Travel Journal

i ♥ NYC

Date _____

Place to Explore

Things to See & Do :

- [ ] ....
- [ ] ....
- [ ] ....
- [ ] ....
- [ ] ....
- [ ] ....
- [ ] ....
- [ ] ....
- [ ] ....
- [ ] ....

Things to Observe :

- [ ] _____
- [ ] _____
- [ ] _____
- [ ] _____
- [ ] _____
- [ ] _____
- [ ] _____

Places to Mingle :

- [ ] _____
- [ ] _____
- [ ] _____
- [ ] _____
- [ ] _____
- [ ] _____
- [ ] _____

Adventure to Have :

- [ ] _____
- [ ] _____
- [ ] _____
- [ ] _____
- [ ] _____
- [ ] _____
- [ ] _____

Travel Journal

i ♥ NYC

Sreets to Check Out :

- ☐ _____
- ☐ _____
- ☐ _____
- ☐ _____
- ☐ _____
- ☐ _____
- ☐ _____

People to Meet :

- ☐ _____
- ☐ _____
- ☐ _____
- ☐ _____
- ☐ _____
- ☐ _____
- ☐ _____

Shops to Visit :

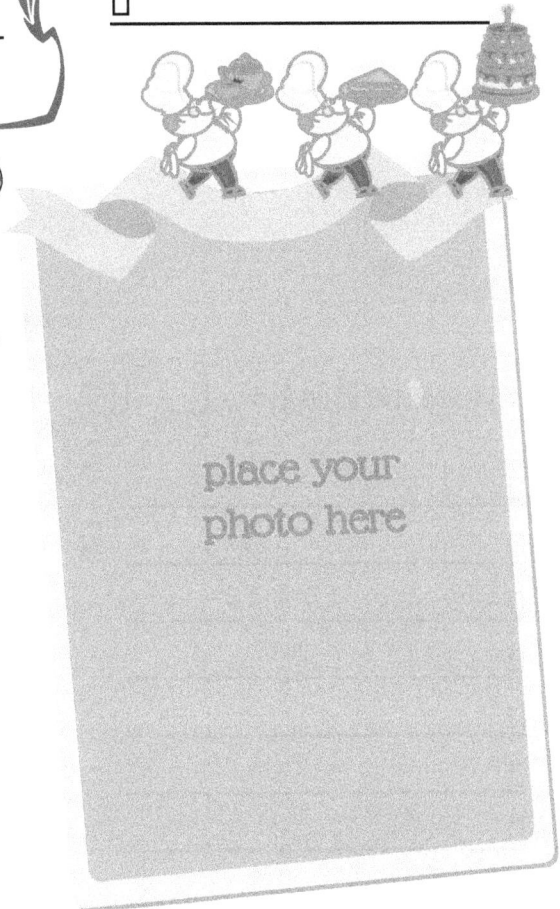

- ☐ _____
- ☐ _____
- ☐ _____
- ☐ _____
- ☐ _____
- ☐ _____
- ☐ _____

place your
photo here

Travel Journal

Date _____

_____
Place to Explore

i ♥ NYC

Things to See & Do :

- ☐ ....
- ☐ ....
- ☐ ....
- ☐ ....
- ☐ ....
- ☐ ....
- ☐ ....
- ☐ ....
- ☐ ....
- ☐ ....

Things to Observe :

- ☐ _____
- ☐ _____
- ☐ _____
- ☐ _____
- ☐ _____
- ☐ _____
- ☐ _____

Places to Mingle :

- ☐ _____
- ☐ _____
- ☐ _____
- ☐ _____
- ☐ _____
- ☐ _____
- ☐ _____

Adventure to Have :

- ☐ _____
- ☐ _____
- ☐ _____
- ☐ _____
- ☐ _____
- ☐ _____
- ☐ _____

Travel Journal

i
♥
NYC

Sreets to Check Out :

- ☐ _____
- ☐ _____
- ☐ _____
- ☐ _____
- ☐ _____
- ☐ _____
- ☐ _____

People to Meet :

- ☐ _____
- ☐ _____
- ☐ _____
- ☐ _____
- ☐ _____
- ☐ _____
- ☐ _____

place your
photo here

Shops to Visit :

- ☐ _____
- ☐ _____
- ☐ _____
- ☐ _____
- ☐ _____
- ☐ _____
- ☐ _____

Travel Journal

Date _____

_____
Place to Explore

i
♥
NYC

Things to See & Do :

- ☐ ....
- ☐ ....
- ☐ ....
- ☐ ....
- ☐ ....
- ☐ ....
- ☐ ....
- ☐ ....
- ☐ ....
- ☐ ....

Things to Observe :

- ☐ _____
- ☐ _____
- ☐ _____
- ☐ _____
- ☐ _____
- ☐ _____
- ☐ _____

Places to Mingle :

- ☐ _____
- ☐ _____
- ☐ _____
- ☐ _____
- ☐ _____
- ☐ _____
- ☐ _____

Adventure to Have :

- ☐ _____
- ☐ _____
- ☐ _____
- ☐ _____
- ☐ _____
- ☐ _____
- ☐ _____

Travel Journal

Sreets to Check Out :

- [ ] _____
- [ ] _____
- [ ] _____
- [ ] _____
- [ ] _____
- [ ] _____
- [ ] _____

People to Meet :

- [ ] _____
- [ ] _____
- [ ] _____
- [ ] _____
- [ ] _____
- [ ] _____
- [ ] _____

Shops to Visit :

- [ ] _____
- [ ] _____
- [ ] _____
- [ ] _____
- [ ] _____
- [ ] _____
- [ ] _____

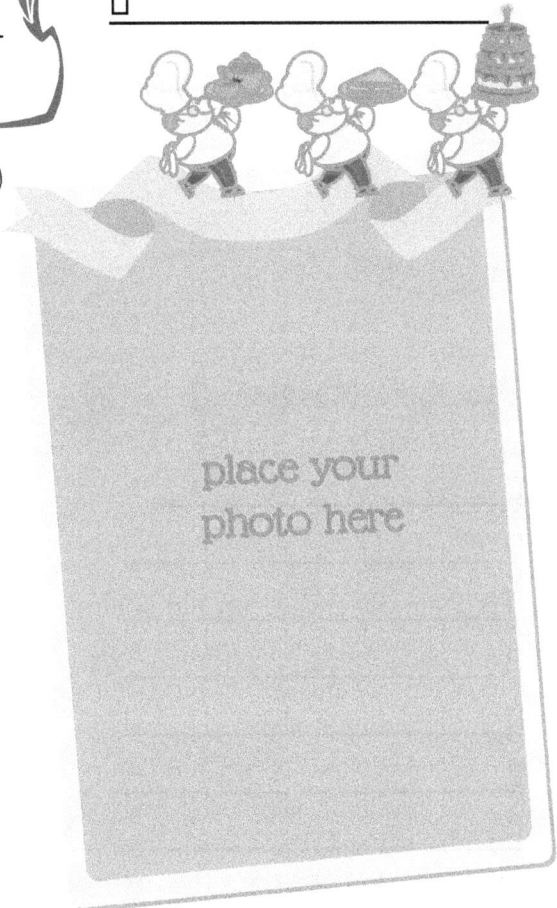

place your
photo here

Travel Journal

Date _____

_____
Place to Explore

i ♥ NYC

Things to See & Do :

- ☐ ....
- ☐ ....
- ☐ ....
- ☐ ....
- ☐ ....
- ☐ ....
- ☐ ....
- ☐ ....
- ☐ ....

Things to Observe :

- ☐ _____
- ☐ _____
- ☐ _____
- ☐ _____
- ☐ _____
- ☐ _____
- ☐ _____

Places to Mingle : 🍴♡🍴

- ☐ _____
- ☐ _____
- ☐ _____
- ☐ _____
- ☐ _____
- ☐ _____
- ☐ _____

Adventure to Have :

- ☐ _____
- ☐ _____
- ☐ _____
- ☐ _____
- ☐ _____
- ☐ _____
- ☐ _____

Travel Journal

i ♥ NYC

Sreets to Check Out :

☐ _____
☐ _____
☐ _____
☐ _____
☐ _____
☐ _____
☐ _____

People to Meet :

☐ _____
☐ _____
☐ _____
☐ _____
☐ _____
☐ _____
☐ _____

Shops to Visit :

☐ _____
☐ _____
☐ _____
☐ _____
☐ _____
☐ _____
☐ _____

place your photo here

Travel Journal

Date _____

_____
Place to Explore

i
♥
NYC

Things to See & Do :

- ☐ ....
- ☐ ....
- ☐ ....
- ☐ ....
- ☐ ....
- ☐ ....
- ☐ ....
- ☐ ....
- ☐ ....
- ☐ ....

Things to Observe :

- ☐ _____
- ☐ _____
- ☐ _____
- ☐ _____
- ☐ _____
- ☐ _____
- ☐ _____

Adventure to Have :

- ☐ _____
- ☐ _____
- ☐ _____
- ☐ _____
- ☐ _____
- ☐ _____

Places to Mingle :

- ☐ _____
- ☐ _____
- ☐ _____
- ☐ _____
- ☐ _____
- ☐ _____
- ☐ _____

Travel Journal

i ♥ NYC

Sreets to Check Out :

- ☐ _____
- ☐ _____
- ☐ _____
- ☐ _____
- ☐ _____
- ☐ _____
- ☐ _____

People to Meet :

- ☐ _____
- ☐ _____
- ☐ _____
- ☐ _____
- ☐ _____
- ☐ _____
- ☐ _____

Shops to Visit :

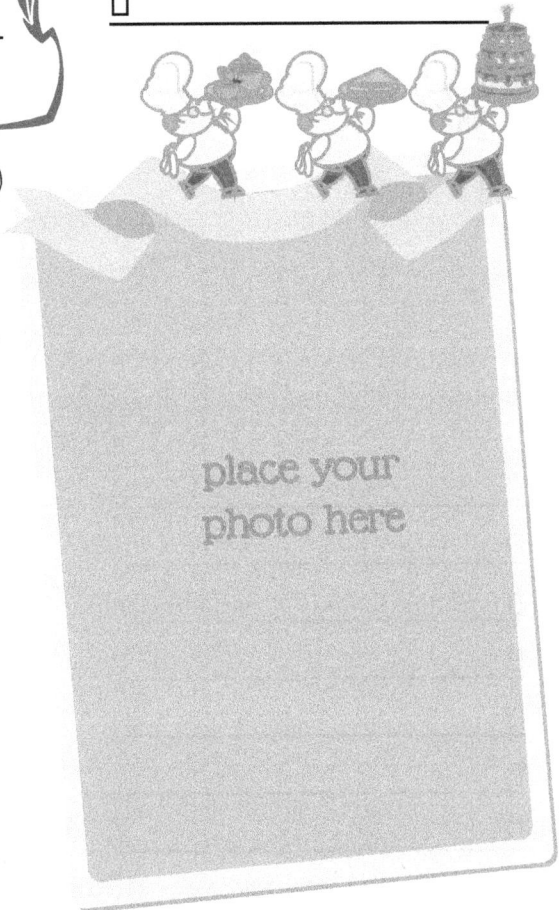

- ☐ _____
- ☐ _____
- ☐ _____
- ☐ _____
- ☐ _____
- ☐ _____
- ☐ _____

place your photo here

Travel Journal

Date _____

_____
Place to Explore

i
♥
NYC

Things to See & Do :

☐ ....
☐ ....
☐ ....
☐ ....
☐ ....
☐ ....
☐ ....
☐ ....
☐ ....

Things to Observe :

☐ _____
☐ _____
☐ _____
☐ _____
☐ _____
☐ _____
☐ _____

Places to Mingle :

☐ _____
☐ _____
☐ _____
☐ _____
☐ _____
☐ _____
☐ _____

Adventure to Have :

☐ _____
☐ _____
☐ _____
☐ _____
☐ _____
☐ _____
☐ _____

Travel Journal

i ♥ NYC

Sreets to Check Out :

- ☐ _____
- ☐ _____
- ☐ _____
- ☐ _____
- ☐ _____
- ☐ _____
- ☐ _____

People to Meet :

- ☐ _____
- ☐ _____
- ☐ _____
- ☐ _____
- ☐ _____
- ☐ _____
- ☐ _____

Shops to Visit :

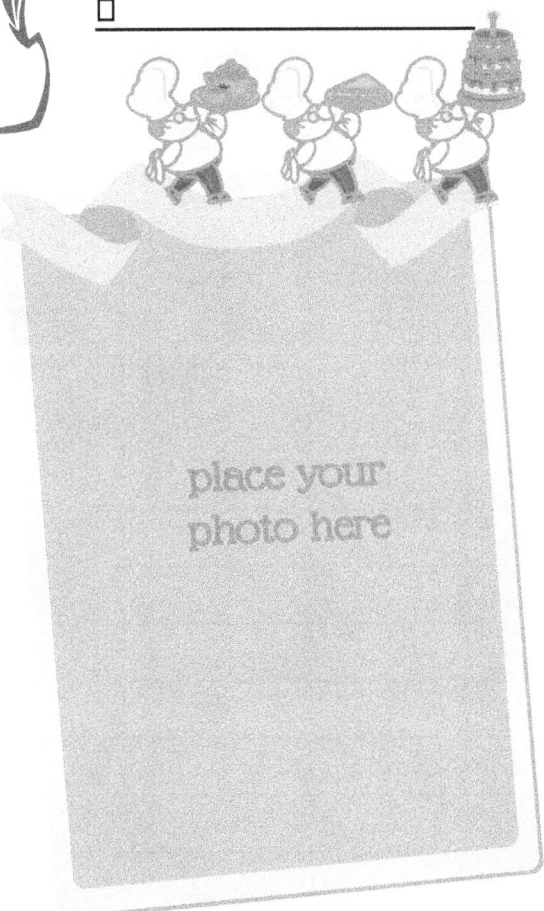

- ☐ _____
- ☐ _____
- ☐ _____
- ☐ _____
- ☐ _____
- ☐ _____
- ☐ _____

place your photo here

Travel Journal

Date _____

_____
Place to Explore

i ♥ NYC

Things to See & Do :

- ☐ ....
- ☐ ....
- ☐ ....
- ☐ ....
- ☐ ....
- ☐ ....
- ☐ ....
- ☐ ....
- ☐ ....
- ☐ ....

Things to Observe :

- ☐ _____
- ☐ _____
- ☐ _____
- ☐ _____
- ☐ _____
- ☐ _____
- ☐ _____

Places to Mingle :

- ☐ _____
- ☐ _____
- ☐ _____
- ☐ _____
- ☐ _____
- ☐ _____
- ☐ _____

Adventure to Have :

- ☐ _____
- ☐ _____
- ☐ _____
- ☐ _____
- ☐ _____
- ☐ _____
- ☐ _____

Travel Journal

i ♥ NYC

Sreets to Check Out :

☐ _____
☐ _____
☐ _____
☐ _____
☐ _____
☐ _____
☐ _____

People to Meet :

☐ _____
☐ _____
☐ _____
☐ _____
☐ _____
☐ _____
☐ _____

Shops to Visit :

☐ _____
☐ _____
☐ _____
☐ _____
☐ _____
☐ _____
☐ _____

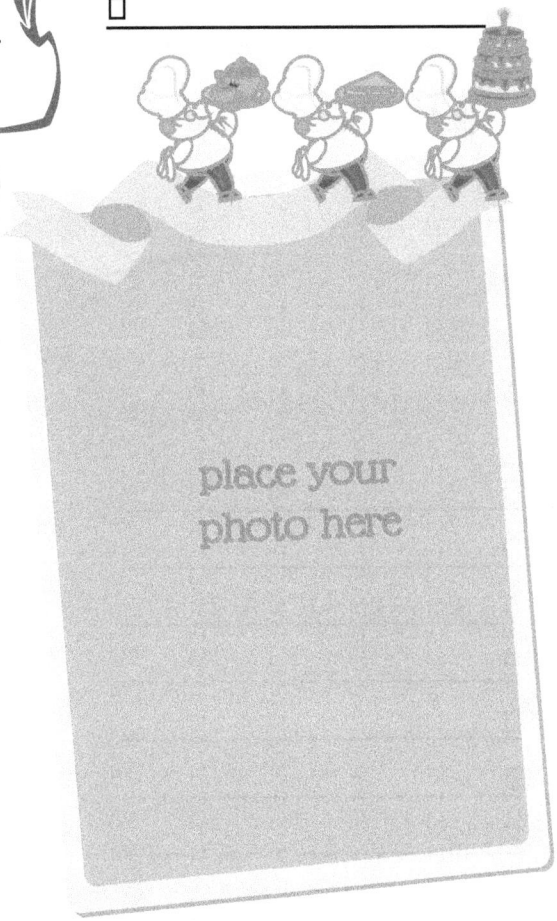

place your photo here

Travel Journal

Date _____

_____
Place to Explore

i
♥
NYC

Things to See & Do :

☐ ....
☐ ....
☐ ....
☐ ....
☐ ....
☐ ....
☐ ....
☐ ....
☐ ....

Things to Observe :

☐ _____
☐ _____
☐ _____
☐ _____
☐ _____
☐ _____
☐ _____

Places to Mingle :

☐ _____
☐ _____
☐ _____
☐ _____
☐ _____
☐ _____
☐ _____

Adventure to Have :

☐ _____
☐ _____
☐ _____
☐ _____
☐ _____
☐ _____
☐ _____

Travel Journal

i ♥ NYC

Sreets to Check Out :

- ☐ _____
- ☐ _____
- ☐ _____
- ☐ _____
- ☐ _____
- ☐ _____
- ☐ _____

People to Meet :

- ☐ _____
- ☐ _____
- ☐ _____
- ☐ _____
- ☐ _____
- ☐ _____
- ☐ _____

Shops to Visit :

- ☐ _____
- ☐ _____
- ☐ _____
- ☐ _____
- ☐ _____
- ☐ _____
- ☐ _____

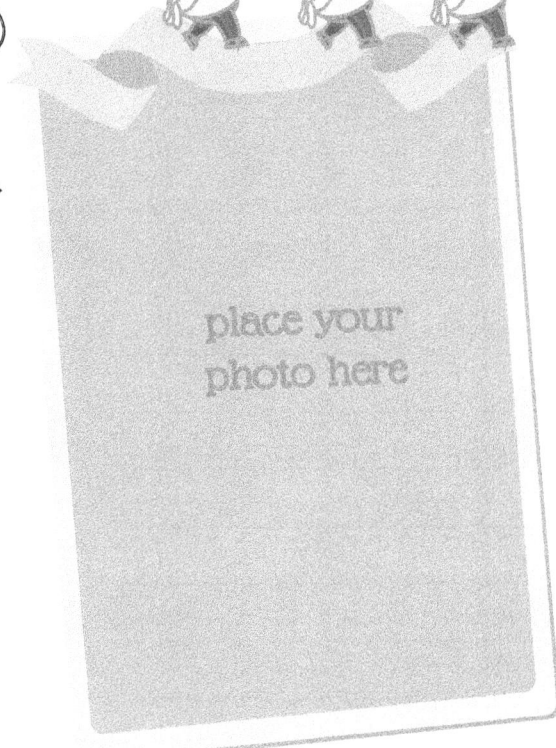
place your photo here

Travel Journal

i ♥ NYC

Date _____

_____
Place to Explore

Things to See & Do :

- ☐ ....
- ☐ ....
- ☐ ....
- ☐ ....
- ☐ ....
- ☐ ....
- ☐ ....
- ☐ ....
- ☐ ....
- ☐ ....

Things to Observe :

- ☐ _____
- ☐ _____
- ☐ _____
- ☐ _____
- ☐ _____
- ☐ _____
- ☐ _____

Places to Mingle :

- ☐ _____
- ☐ _____
- ☐ _____
- ☐ _____
- ☐ _____
- ☐ _____
- ☐ _____

Adventure to Have :

- ☐ _____
- ☐ _____
- ☐ _____
- ☐ _____
- ☐ _____
- ☐ _____
- ☐ _____

Travel Journal

i ♥ NYC

Sreets to Check Out :

- ☐ _____
- ☐ _____
- ☐ _____
- ☐ _____
- ☐ _____
- ☐ _____
- ☐ _____

People to Meet :

- ☐ _____
- ☐ _____
- ☐ _____
- ☐ _____
- ☐ _____
- ☐ _____
- ☐ _____

Shops to Visit :

- ☐ _____
- ☐ _____
- ☐ _____
- ☐ _____
- ☐ _____
- ☐ _____
- ☐ _____

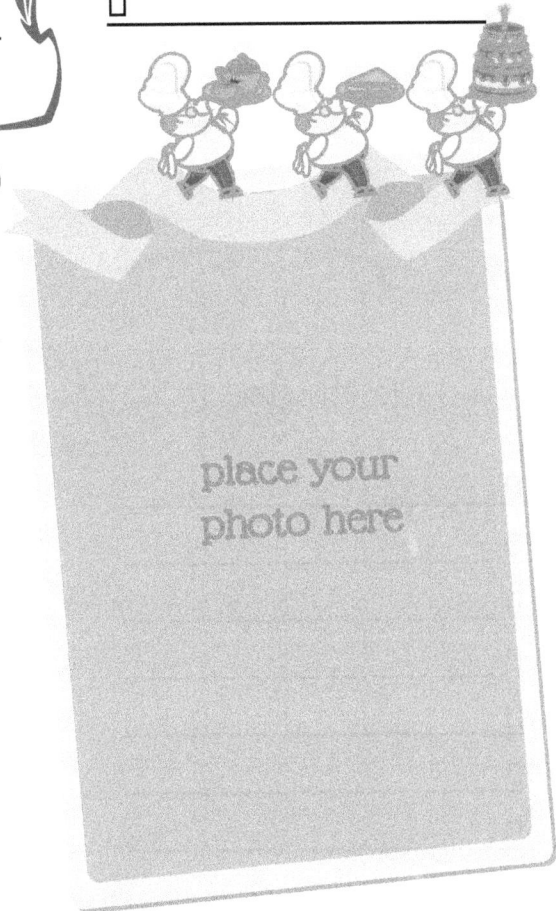
place your photo here

Travel Journal

i ♥ NYC

Date _____ _____

Place to Explore

Things to See & Do :

- ☐ ....
- ☐ ....
- ☐ ....
- ☐ ....
- ☐ ....
- ☐ ....
- ☐ ....
- ☐ ....
- ☐ ....
- ☐ ....

Things to Observe :

- ☐ _____
- ☐ _____
- ☐ _____
- ☐ _____
- ☐ _____
- ☐ _____
- ☐ _____

Places to Mingle : 🍴♡🍴

- ☐ _____
- ☐ _____
- ☐ _____
- ☐ _____
- ☐ _____
- ☐ _____
- ☐ _____

Adventure to Have :

- ☐ _____
- ☐ _____
- ☐ _____
- ☐ _____
- ☐ _____
- ☐ _____
- ☐ _____

Travel Journal

i ♥ NYC

Sreets to Check Out :

- ☐ _____
- ☐ _____
- ☐ _____
- ☐ _____
- ☐ _____
- ☐ _____
- ☐ _____

People to Meet :

- ☐ _____
- ☐ _____
- ☐ _____
- ☐ _____
- ☐ _____
- ☐ _____
- ☐ _____

Shops to Visit :

- ☐ _____
- ☐ _____
- ☐ _____
- ☐ _____
- ☐ _____
- ☐ _____
- ☐ _____

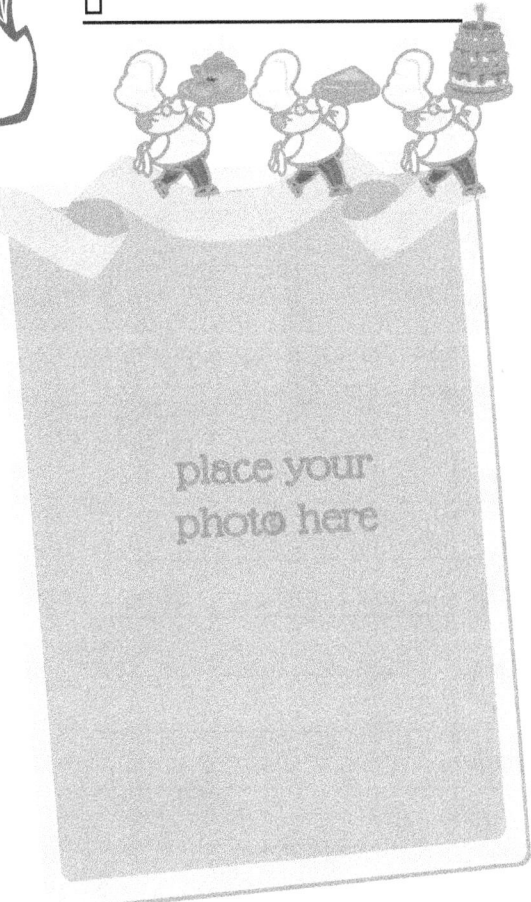

place your
photo here

Travel Journal

Date _____

Place to Explore

i ♥ NYC

Things to See & Do :

- ☐ ....
- ☐ ....
- ☐ ....
- ☐ ....
- ☐ ....
- ☐ ....
- ☐ ....
- ☐ ....
- ☐ ....
- ☐ ....

Things to Observe :

- ☐ _____
- ☐ _____
- ☐ _____
- ☐ _____
- ☐ _____
- ☐ _____
- ☐ _____

Places to Mingle :

- ☐ _____
- ☐ _____
- ☐ _____
- ☐ _____
- ☐ _____
- ☐ _____
- ☐ _____

Adventure to Have :

- ☐ _____
- ☐ _____
- ☐ _____
- ☐ _____
- ☐ _____
- ☐ _____
- ☐ _____

Travel Journal

i ♥ NYC

Sreets to Check Out :

- ☐ _____
- ☐ _____
- ☐ _____
- ☐ _____
- ☐ _____
- ☐ _____
- ☐ _____

People to Meet :

- ☐ _____
- ☐ _____
- ☐ _____
- ☐ _____
- ☐ _____
- ☐ _____
- ☐ _____

Shops to Visit :

- ☐ _____
- ☐ _____
- ☐ _____
- ☐ _____
- ☐ _____
- ☐ _____
- ☐ _____

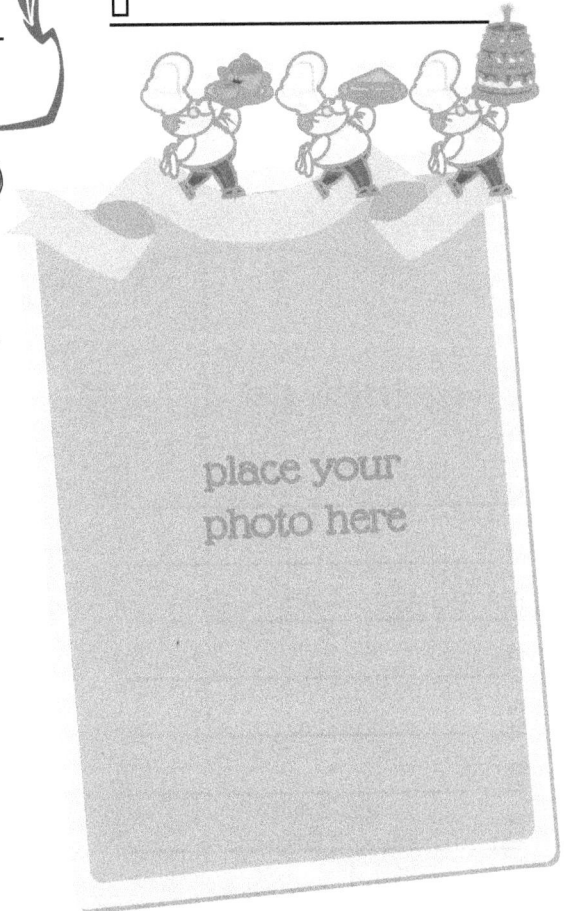

place your photo here

Travel Journal

Date _____

Place to Explore
_____

i ♥ NYC

Things to See & Do :

☐ ....
☐ ....
☐ ....
☐ ....
☐ ....
☐ ....
☐ ....
☐ ....
☐ ....

Things to Observe :

☐ _____
☐ _____
☐ _____
☐ _____
☐ _____
☐ _____
☐ _____

Places to Mingle :

☐ _____
☐ _____
☐ _____
☐ _____
☐ _____
☐ _____
☐ _____

Adventure to Have :

☐ _____
☐ _____
☐ _____
☐ _____
☐ _____
☐ _____
☐ _____

Travel Journal

i ♥ NYC

Sreets to Check Out :

- ☐ _____
- ☐ _____
- ☐ _____
- ☐ _____
- ☐ _____
- ☐ _____
- ☐ _____

People to Meet :

- ☐ _____
- ☐ _____
- ☐ _____
- ☐ _____
- ☐ _____
- ☐ _____
- ☐ _____

Shops to Visit :

- ☐ _____
- ☐ _____
- ☐ _____
- ☐ _____
- ☐ _____
- ☐ _____
- ☐ _____

place your photo here

Travel Journal

i ♥ NYC

Date _____

_____
Place to Explore

Things to See & Do :

- ☐ ....
- ☐ ....
- ☐ ....
- ☐ ....
- ☐ ....
- ☐ ....
- ☐ ....
- ☐ ....
- ☐ ....
- ☐ ....

Things to Observe :

- ☐ _____
- ☐ _____
- ☐ _____
- ☐ _____
- ☐ _____
- ☐ _____
- ☐ _____

Places to Mingle :

- ☐ _____
- ☐ _____
- ☐ _____
- ☐ _____
- ☐ _____
- ☐ _____
- ☐ _____

Adventure to Have :

- ☐ _____
- ☐ _____
- ☐ _____
- ☐ _____
- ☐ _____
- ☐ _____
- ☐ _____

Travel Journal

i ♥ NYC

Sreets to Check Out :

☐ _____
☐ _____
☐ _____
☐ _____
☐ _____
☐ _____
☐ _____

People to Meet :

☐ _____
☐ _____
☐ _____
☐ _____
☐ _____
☐ _____
☐ _____

Shops to Visit :

☐ _____
☐ _____
☐ _____
☐ _____
☐ _____
☐ _____
☐ _____

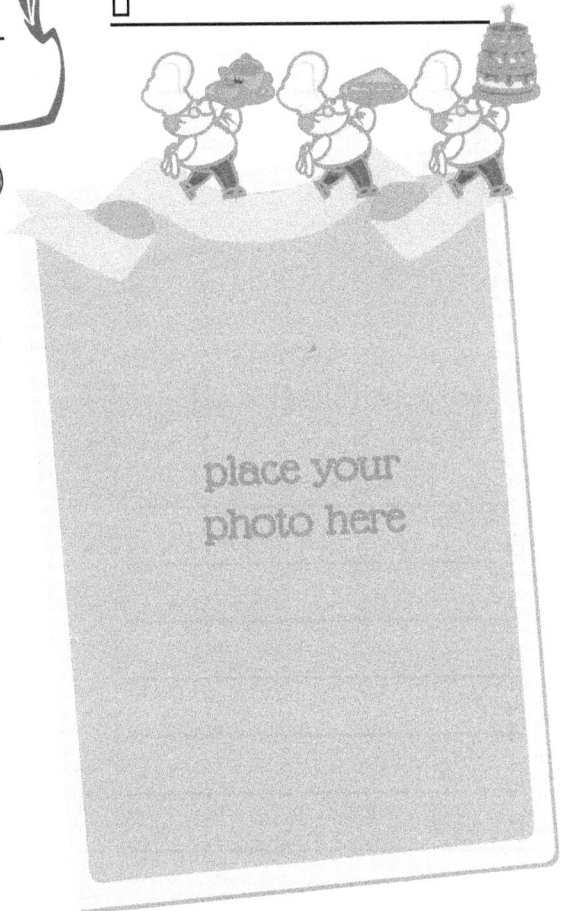

place your
photo here

Travel Journal

i ♥ NYC

Date _____

Place to Explore

Things to See & Do :

☐ ....
☐ ....
☐ ....
☐ ....
☐ ....
☐ ....
☐ ....
☐ ....
☐ ....
☐ ....

Things to Observe :

☐ _____
☐ _____
☐ _____
☐ _____
☐ _____
☐ _____
☐ _____

Places to Mingle :

☐ _____
☐ _____
☐ _____
☐ _____
☐ _____
☐ _____
☐ _____

Adventure to Have :

☐ _____
☐ _____
☐ _____
☐ _____
☐ _____
☐ _____
☐ _____

Travel Journal

i ♥ NYC

Sreets to Check Out :

☐ _____
☐ _____
☐ _____
☐ _____
☐ _____
☐ _____
☐ _____

People to Meet :

☐ _____
☐ _____
☐ _____
☐ _____
☐ _____
☐ _____
☐ _____

place your photo here

Shops to Visit :

☐ _____
☐ _____
☐ _____
☐ _____
☐ _____
☐ _____
☐ _____

Travel Journal

Date _____

_____
Place to Explore

i
♥
NYC

Things to See & Do :

☐ ....
☐ ....
☐ ....
☐ ....
☐ ....
☐ ....
☐ ....
☐ ....
☐ ....

Things to Observe :

☐ _____
☐ _____
☐ _____
☐ _____
☐ _____
☐ _____
☐ _____

Places to Mingle :

☐ _____
☐ _____
☐ _____
☐ _____
☐ _____
☐ _____
☐ _____

Adventure to Have :

☐ _____
☐ _____
☐ _____
☐ _____
☐ _____
☐ _____
☐ _____

Travel Journal

i ♥ NYC

Sreets to Check Out :

- [ ] _____
- [ ] _____
- [ ] _____
- [ ] _____
- [ ] _____
- [ ] _____
- [ ] _____

People to Meet :

- [ ] _____
- [ ] _____
- [ ] _____
- [ ] _____
- [ ] _____
- [ ] _____
- [ ] _____

Shops to Visit :

- [ ] _____
- [ ] _____
- [ ] _____
- [ ] _____
- [ ] _____
- [ ] _____
- [ ] _____

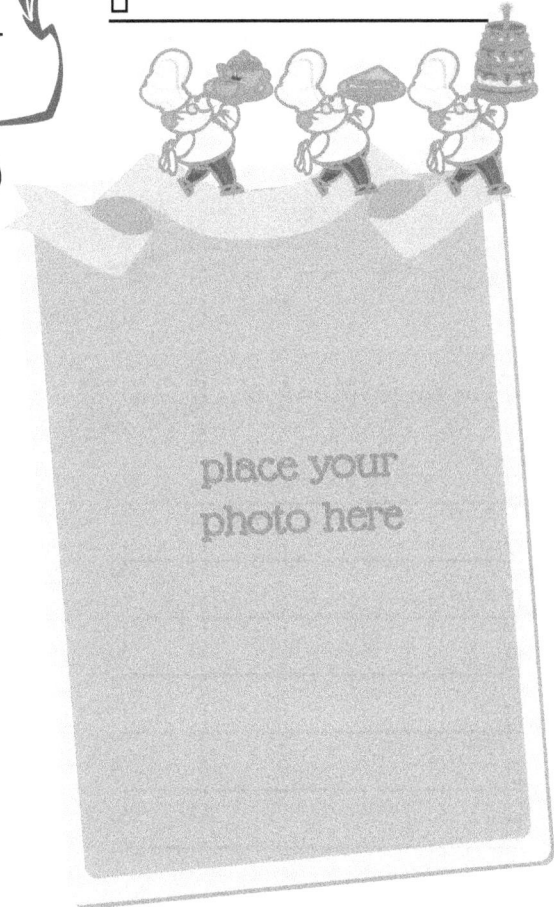

place your photo here

Travel Journal

Date _____

_____
Place to Explore

i
♥
NYC

Things to See & Do :

- ☐ ....
- ☐ ....
- ☐ ....
- ☐ ....
- ☐ ....
- ☐ ....
- ☐ ....
- ☐ ....
- ☐ ....
- ☐ ....

Things to Observe :

- ☐ _____
- ☐ _____
- ☐ _____
- ☐ _____
- ☐ _____
- ☐ _____
- ☐ _____

Places to Mingle :

- ☐ _____
- ☐ _____
- ☐ _____
- ☐ _____
- ☐ _____
- ☐ _____
- ☐ _____

Adventure to Have :

- ☐ _____
- ☐ _____
- ☐ _____
- ☐ _____
- ☐ _____
- ☐ _____
- ☐ _____

Travel Journal

i ♥ NYC

Sreets to Check Out :

- ☐ _____
- ☐ _____
- ☐ _____
- ☐ _____
- ☐ _____
- ☐ _____
- ☐ _____

People to Meet :

- ☐ _____
- ☐ _____
- ☐ _____
- ☐ _____
- ☐ _____
- ☐ _____
- ☐ _____

Shops to Visit :

- ☐ _____
- ☐ _____
- ☐ _____
- ☐ _____
- ☐ _____
- ☐ _____
- ☐ _____

place your photo here

Travel Journal

Date _____

_____
Place to Explore

i ♥ NYC

Things to See & Do :

- ☐ ....
- ☐ ....
- ☐ ....
- ☐ ....
- ☐ ....
- ☐ ....
- ☐ ....
- ☐ ....
- ☐ ....
- ☐ ....

Things to Observe :

- ☐ _____
- ☐ _____
- ☐ _____
- ☐ _____
- ☐ _____
- ☐ _____
- ☐ _____

Places to Mingle : 🍴♡🍴

- ☐ _____
- ☐ _____
- ☐ _____
- ☐ _____
- ☐ _____
- ☐ _____
- ☐ _____

Adventure to Have :

- ☐ _____
- ☐ _____
- ☐ _____
- ☐ _____
- ☐ _____
- ☐ _____

Travel Journal

i ♥ NYC

Sreets to Check Out :

- ☐ _____
- ☐ _____
- ☐ _____
- ☐ _____
- ☐ _____
- ☐ _____
- ☐ _____

People to Meet :

- ☐ _____
- ☐ _____
- ☐ _____
- ☐ _____
- ☐ _____
- ☐ _____
- ☐ _____

Shops to Visit :

- ☐ _____
- ☐ _____
- ☐ _____
- ☐ _____
- ☐ _____
- ☐ _____
- ☐ _____

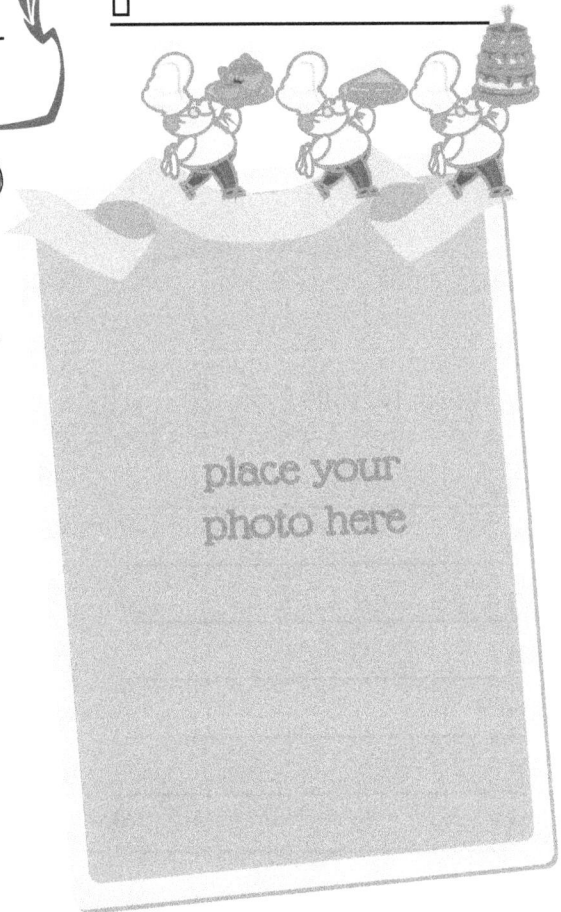

place your photo here

Travel Journal

Date _____

Place to Explore

i ♥ NYC

Things to See & Do :

☐ ....
☐ ....
☐ ....
☐ ....
☐ ....
☐ ....
☐ ....
☐ ....
☐ ....
☐ ....

Things to Observe :

☐ _____
☐ _____
☐ _____
☐ _____
☐ _____
☐ _____
☐ _____

Places to Mingle :

☐ _____
☐ _____
☐ _____
☐ _____
☐ _____
☐ _____
☐ _____

Adventure to Have :

☐ _____
☐ _____
☐ _____
☐ _____
☐ _____
☐ _____
☐ _____

Travel Journal

i ♥ NYC

Sreets to Check Out :

- ☐ _____
- ☐ _____
- ☐ _____
- ☐ _____
- ☐ _____
- ☐ _____
- ☐ _____

People to Meet :

- ☐ _____
- ☐ _____
- ☐ _____
- ☐ _____
- ☐ _____
- ☐ _____
- ☐ _____

Shops to Visit :

- ☐ _____
- ☐ _____
- ☐ _____
- ☐ _____
- ☐ _____
- ☐ _____
- ☐ _____

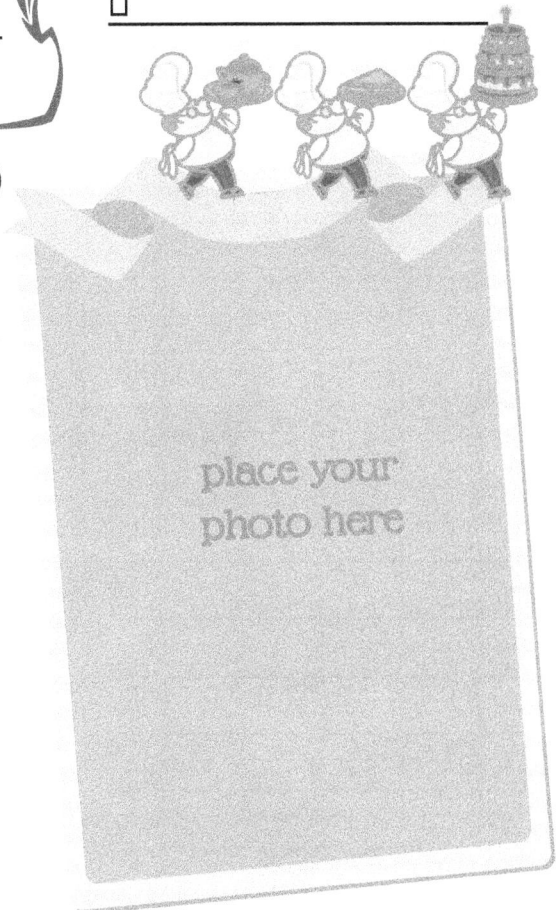

place your photo here

Travel Journal

i ♥ NYC

Date _____

_____
Place to Explore

Things to See & Do :

- ☐ ....
- ☐ ....
- ☐ ....
- ☐ ....
- ☐ ....
- ☐ ....
- ☐ ....
- ☐ ....
- ☐ ....
- ☐ ....

Things to Observe :

- ☐ _____
- ☐ _____
- ☐ _____
- ☐ _____
- ☐ _____
- ☐ _____
- ☐ _____

Places to Mingle : 🍽♡🍴

- ☐ _____
- ☐ _____
- ☐ _____
- ☐ _____
- ☐ _____
- ☐ _____
- ☐ _____

Adventure to Have :

- ☐ _____
- ☐ _____
- ☐ _____
- ☐ _____
- ☐ _____
- ☐ _____
- ☐ _____

Travel Journal

i ♥ NYC

Sreets to Check Out :

- ☐ _____
- ☐ _____
- ☐ _____
- ☐ _____
- ☐ _____
- ☐ _____
- ☐ _____

People to Meet :

- ☐ _____
- ☐ _____
- ☐ _____
- ☐ _____
- ☐ _____
- ☐ _____
- ☐ _____

Shops to Visit :

- ☐ _____
- ☐ _____
- ☐ _____
- ☐ _____
- ☐ _____
- ☐ _____
- ☐ _____

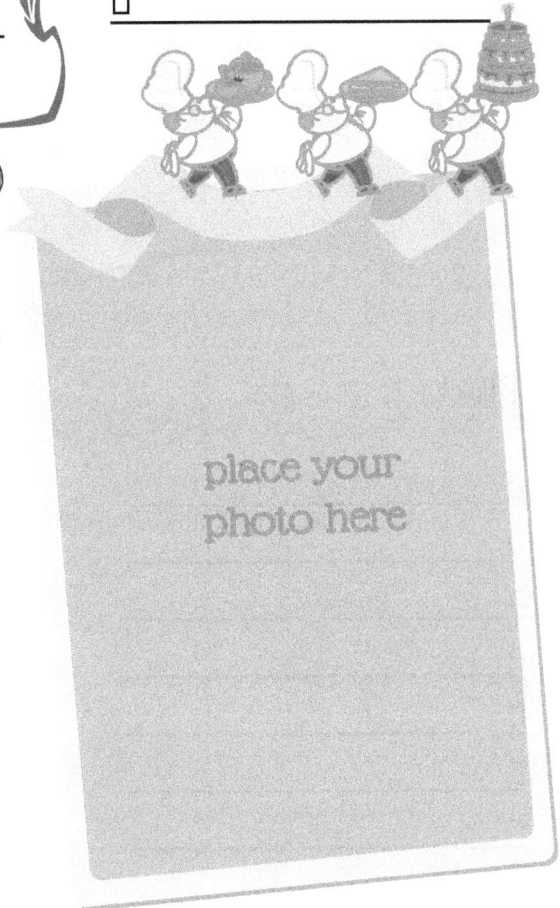

place your photo here

Travel Journal

Date _____

_____
Place to Explore

i ♥ NYC

Things to See & Do :

☐ ....
☐ ....
☐ ....
☐ ....
☐ ....
☐ ....
☐ ....
☐ ....
☐ ....

Things to Observe :

☐ _____
☐ _____
☐ _____
☐ _____
☐ _____
☐ _____
☐ _____

Places to Mingle :

☐ _____
☐ _____
☐ _____
☐ _____
☐ _____
☐ _____
☐ _____

Adventure to Have :

☐ _____
☐ _____
☐ _____
☐ _____
☐ _____
☐ _____
☐ _____

Travel Journal

Sreets to Check Out :

- ☐ _____
- ☐ _____
- ☐ _____
- ☐ _____
- ☐ _____
- ☐ _____
- ☐ _____

People to Meet :

- ☐ _____
- ☐ _____
- ☐ _____
- ☐ _____
- ☐ _____
- ☐ _____
- ☐ _____

Shops to Visit :

- ☐ _____
- ☐ _____
- ☐ _____
- ☐ _____
- ☐ _____
- ☐ _____
- ☐ _____

place your
photo here

Travel Journal

Date _____

_____
Place to Explore

i ♥ NYC

Things to See & Do :

- ☐ ....
- ☐ ....
- ☐ ....
- ☐ ....
- ☐ ....
- ☐ ....
- ☐ ....
- ☐ ....
- ☐ ....
- ☐ ....

Things to Observe :

- ☐ _____
- ☐ _____
- ☐ _____
- ☐ _____
- ☐ _____
- ☐ _____
- ☐ _____

Places to Mingle : 🍽

- ☐ _____
- ☐ _____
- ☐ _____
- ☐ _____
- ☐ _____
- ☐ _____
- ☐ _____

Adventure to Have :

- ☐ _____
- ☐ _____
- ☐ _____
- ☐ _____
- ☐ _____
- ☐ _____

Travel Journal

I ♥ NYC

Sreets to Check Out :

☐ _____
☐ _____
☐ _____
☐ _____
☐ _____
☐ _____
☐ _____

People to Meet :

☐ _____
☐ _____
☐ _____
☐ _____
☐ _____
☐ _____
☐ _____

Shops to Visit :

☐ _____
☐ _____
☐ _____
☐ _____
☐ _____
☐ _____
☐ _____

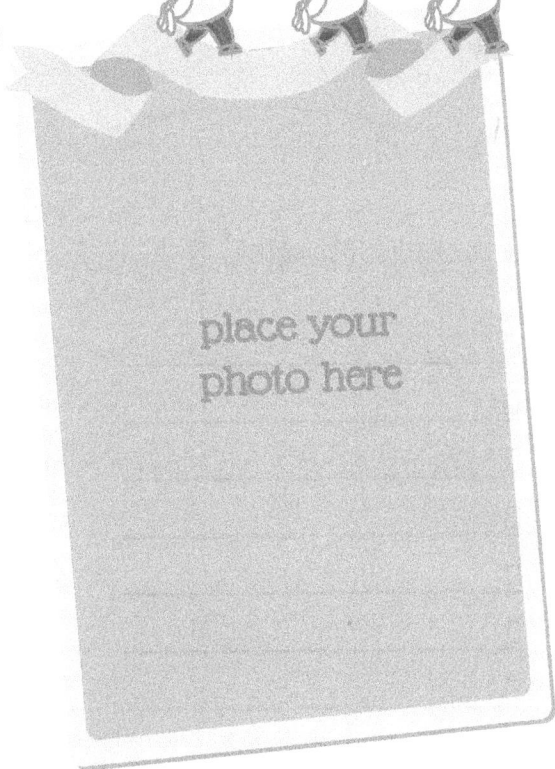

place your photo here

Travel Journal

Date _____

Place to Explore

i ♥ NYC

Things to See & Do :

- ☐ ....
- ☐ ....
- ☐ ....
- ☐ ....
- ☐ ....
- ☐ ....
- ☐ ....
- ☐ ....
- ☐ ....
- ☐ ....

Things to Observe :

- ☐ _____
- ☐ _____
- ☐ _____
- ☐ _____
- ☐ _____
- ☐ _____
- ☐ _____

Places to Mingle : 🍴♥🍴

- ☐ _____
- ☐ _____
- ☐ _____
- ☐ _____
- ☐ _____
- ☐ _____
- ☐ _____

Adventure to Have :

- ☐ _____
- ☐ _____
- ☐ _____
- ☐ _____
- ☐ _____
- ☐ _____
- ☐ _____

Travel Journal

i ♥ NYC

Sreets to Check Out :

- ☐ _____
- ☐ _____
- ☐ _____
- ☐ _____
- ☐ _____
- ☐ _____
- ☐ _____

People to Meet :

- ☐ _____
- ☐ _____
- ☐ _____
- ☐ _____
- ☐ _____
- ☐ _____
- ☐ _____

Shops to Visit :

- ☐ _____
- ☐ _____
- ☐ _____
- ☐ _____
- ☐ _____
- ☐ _____
- ☐ _____

place your
photo here

Travel Journal

i ♥ NYC

Date _____

_____
Place to Explore

Things to See & Do :

- ☐ ....
- ☐ ....
- ☐ ....
- ☐ ....
- ☐ ....
- ☐ ....
- ☐ ....
- ☐ ....
- ☐ ....
- ☐ ....

Things to Observe :

- ☐ _____
- ☐ _____
- ☐ _____
- ☐ _____
- ☐ _____
- ☐ _____
- ☐ _____

Places to Mingle : 🍴♡🍴

- ☐ _____
- ☐ _____
- ☐ _____
- ☐ _____
- ☐ _____
- ☐ _____
- ☐ _____

Adventure to Have :

- ☐ _____
- ☐ _____
- ☐ _____
- ☐ _____
- ☐ _____
- ☐ _____

Travel Journal

i ❤ NYC

Sreets to Check Out :

- ☐ _____
- ☐ _____
- ☐ _____
- ☐ _____
- ☐ _____
- ☐ _____
- ☐ _____

People to Meet :

- ☐ _____
- ☐ _____
- ☐ _____
- ☐ _____
- ☐ _____
- ☐ _____
- ☐ _____

Shops to Visit :

- ☐ _____
- ☐ _____
- ☐ _____
- ☐ _____
- ☐ _____
- ☐ _____
- ☐ _____

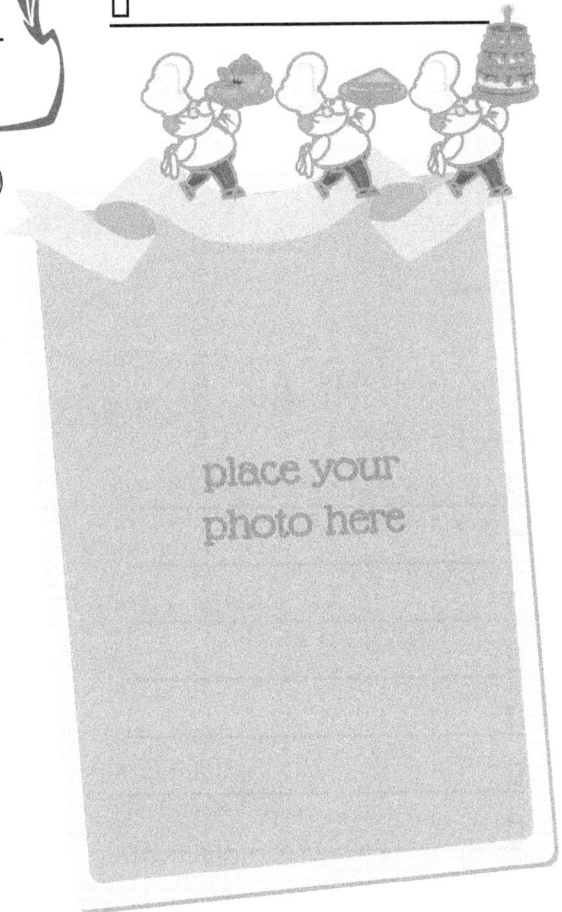
place your photo here

Travel Journal

Date _____

_____
Place to Explore

i ❤ NYC

Things to See & Do :

☐ ....
☐ ....
☐ ....
☐ ....
☐ ....
☐ ....
☐ ....
☐ ....
☐ ....
☐ ....

Things to Observe :

☐ _____
☐ _____
☐ _____
☐ _____
☐ _____
☐ _____
☐ _____

Places to Mingle :

☐ _____
☐ _____
☐ _____
☐ _____
☐ _____
☐ _____
☐ _____

Adventure to Have :

☐ _____
☐ _____
☐ _____
☐ _____
☐ _____
☐ _____

Travel Journal

i ♥ NYC

Sreets to Check Out :

- ☐ _____
- ☐ _____
- ☐ _____
- ☐ _____
- ☐ _____
- ☐ _____
- ☐ _____

People to Meet :

- ☐ _____
- ☐ _____
- ☐ _____
- ☐ _____
- ☐ _____
- ☐ _____
- ☐ _____

Shops to Visit :

- ☐ _____
- ☐ _____
- ☐ _____
- ☐ _____
- ☐ _____
- ☐ _____
- ☐ _____

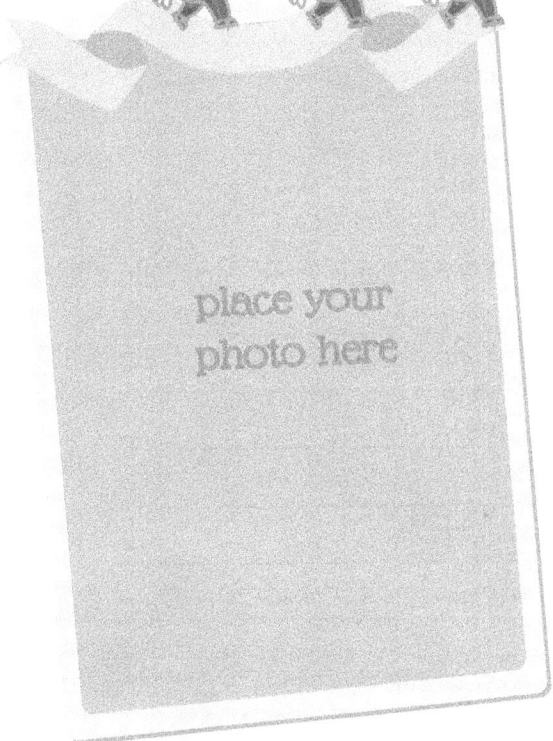

place your photo here

Travel Journal

i ♥ NYC

Date _____

_____
Place to Explore

Things to See & Do :

- ☐ ....
- ☐ ....
- ☐ ....
- ☐ ....
- ☐ ....
- ☐ ....
- ☐ ....
- ☐ ....
- ☐ ....
- ☐ ....

Things to Observe :

- ☐ _____
- ☐ _____
- ☐ _____
- ☐ _____
- ☐ _____
- ☐ _____
- ☐ _____

Places to Mingle :

- ☐ _____
- ☐ _____
- ☐ _____
- ☐ _____
- ☐ _____
- ☐ _____
- ☐ _____

Adventure to Have :

- ☐ _____
- ☐ _____
- ☐ _____
- ☐ _____
- ☐ _____
- ☐ _____
- ☐ _____

Travel Journal

i ♥ NYC

Sreets to Check Out :

☐ _____
☐ _____
☐ _____
☐ _____
☐ _____
☐ _____
☐ _____

People to Meet :

☐ _____
☐ _____
☐ _____
☐ _____
☐ _____
☐ _____
☐ _____

Shops to Visit :

☐ _____
☐ _____
☐ _____
☐ _____
☐ _____
☐ _____
☐ _____

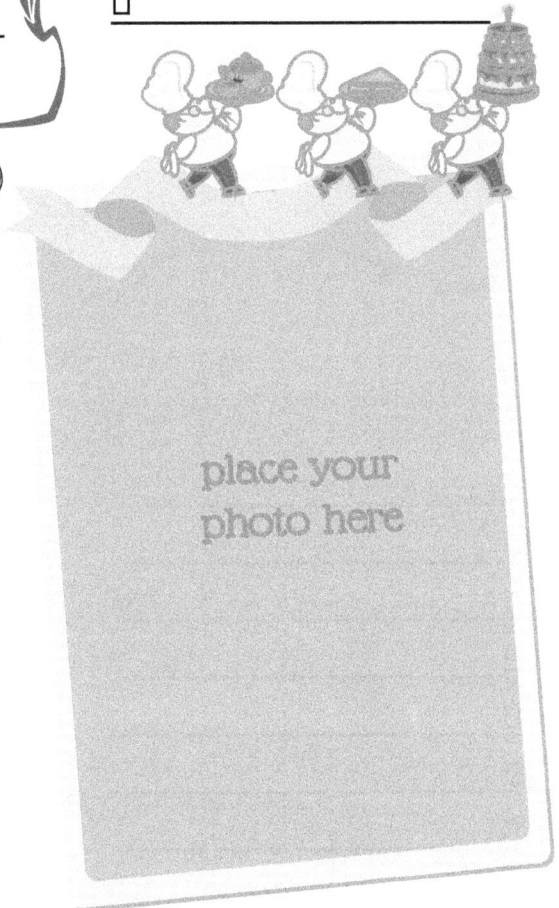
place your photo here

Travel Journal

Date _____

_____
Place to Explore

i
♥
NYC

Things to See & Do :

- ☐ ....
- ☐ ....
- ☐ ....
- ☐ ....
- ☐ ....
- ☐ ....
- ☐ ....
- ☐ ....
- ☐ ....
- ☐ ....

Things to Observe :

- ☐ _____
- ☐ _____
- ☐ _____
- ☐ _____
- ☐ _____
- ☐ _____
- ☐ _____

Places to Mingle :

- ☐ _____
- ☐ _____
- ☐ _____
- ☐ _____
- ☐ _____
- ☐ _____
- ☐ _____

Adventure to Have :

- ☐ _____
- ☐ _____
- ☐ _____
- ☐ _____
- ☐ _____
- ☐ _____
- ☐ _____

Travel Journal

i ♥ NYC

Sreets to Check Out :

- ☐ _____
- ☐ _____
- ☐ _____
- ☐ _____
- ☐ _____
- ☐ _____
- ☐ _____

People to Meet :

- ☐ _____
- ☐ _____
- ☐ _____
- ☐ _____
- ☐ _____
- ☐ _____
- ☐ _____

Shops to Visit :

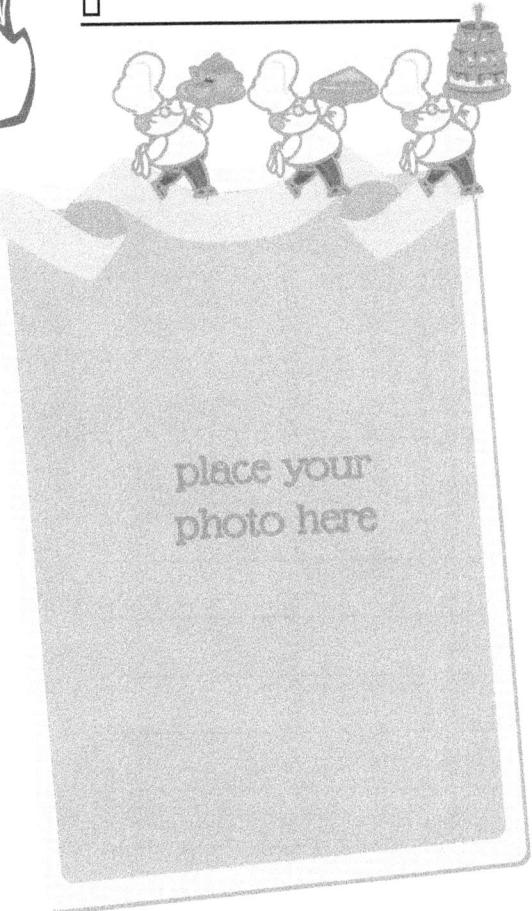

- ☐ _____
- ☐ _____
- ☐ _____
- ☐ _____
- ☐ _____
- ☐ _____
- ☐ _____

place your
photo here

Travel Journal

Date _____

_____
Place to Explore

i
♥
NYC

Things to See & Do :

- ☐ ....
- ☐ ....
- ☐ ....
- ☐ ....
- ☐ ....
- ☐ ....
- ☐ ....
- ☐ ....
- ☐ ....
- ☐ ....

Things to Observe :

- ☐ _____
- ☐ _____
- ☐ _____
- ☐ _____
- ☐ _____
- ☐ _____
- ☐ _____

Places to Mingle :

- ☐ _____
- ☐ _____
- ☐ _____
- ☐ _____
- ☐ _____
- ☐ _____
- ☐ _____

Adventure to Have :

- ☐ _____
- ☐ _____
- ☐ _____
- ☐ _____
- ☐ _____
- ☐ _____
- ☐ _____

Travel Journal

i ♥ NYC

Sreets to Check Out :

☐ _____
☐ _____
☐ _____
☐ _____
☐ _____
☐ _____
☐ _____

People to Meet :

☐ _____
☐ _____
☐ _____
☐ _____
☐ _____
☐ _____
☐ _____

Shops to Visit :

☐ _____
☐ _____
☐ _____
☐ _____
☐ _____
☐ _____
☐ _____

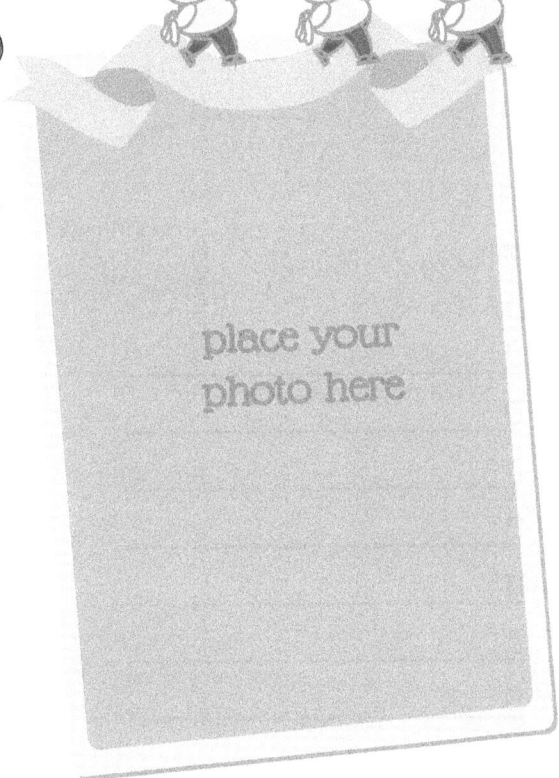

place your photo here

Travel Journal

i ♥ NYC

Date _____

_____
Place to Explore

Things to See & Do :

- ☐ ....
- ☐ ....
- ☐ ....
- ☐ ....
- ☐ ....
- ☐ ....
- ☐ ....
- ☐ ....
- ☐ ....

Things to Observe :

- ☐ _____
- ☐ _____
- ☐ _____
- ☐ _____
- ☐ _____
- ☐ _____
- ☐ _____

Places to Mingle :

- ☐ _____
- ☐ _____
- ☐ _____
- ☐ _____
- ☐ _____
- ☐ _____
- ☐ _____

Adventure to Have :

- ☐ _____
- ☐ _____
- ☐ _____
- ☐ _____
- ☐ _____
- ☐ _____
- ☐ _____

Travel Journal

i ♥ NYC

Sreets to Check Out :

☐ _____
☐ _____
☐ _____
☐ _____
☐ _____
☐ _____
☐ _____

People to Meet :

☐ _____
☐ _____
☐ _____
☐ _____
☐ _____
☐ _____
☐ _____

Shops to Visit :

☐ _____
☐ _____
☐ _____
☐ _____
☐ _____
☐ _____
☐ _____

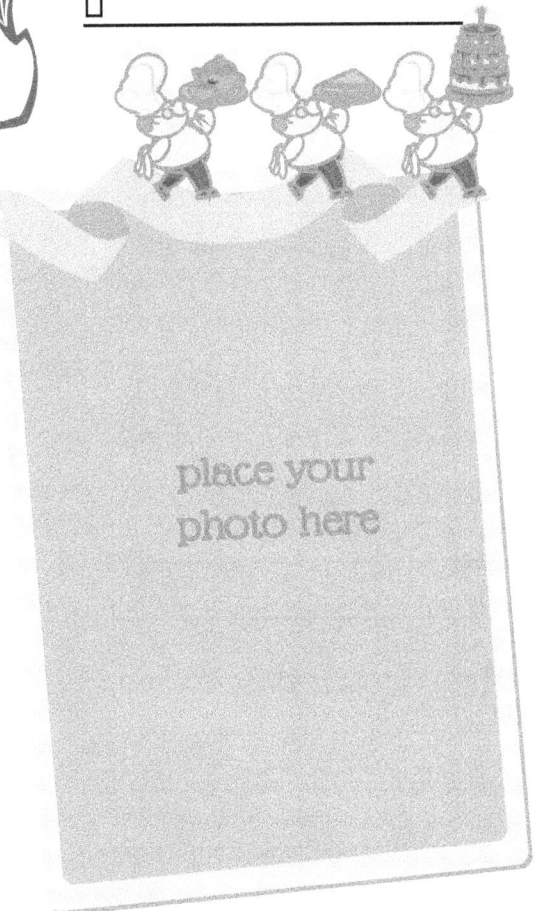
place your photo here

Travel Journal

Date _____

_____
Place to Explore

i ♥ NYC

Things to See & Do :

- ☐ ....
- ☐ ....
- ☐ ....
- ☐ ....
- ☐ ....
- ☐ ....
- ☐ ....
- ☐ ....
- ☐ ....
- ☐ ....

Things to Observe :

- ☐ _____
- ☐ _____
- ☐ _____
- ☐ _____
- ☐ _____
- ☐ _____
- ☐ _____

Places to Mingle :

- ☐ _____
- ☐ _____
- ☐ _____
- ☐ _____
- ☐ _____
- ☐ _____
- ☐ _____

Adventure to Have :

- ☐ _____
- ☐ _____
- ☐ _____
- ☐ _____
- ☐ _____
- ☐ _____
- ☐ _____

Travel Journal

i ♥ NYC

Sreets to Check Out :

- ☐ _____
- ☐ _____
- ☐ _____
- ☐ _____
- ☐ _____
- ☐ _____
- ☐ _____

People to Meet :

- ☐ _____
- ☐ _____
- ☐ _____
- ☐ _____
- ☐ _____
- ☐ _____
- ☐ _____

Shops to Visit :

- ☐ _____
- ☐ _____
- ☐ _____
- ☐ _____
- ☐ _____
- ☐ _____
- ☐ _____

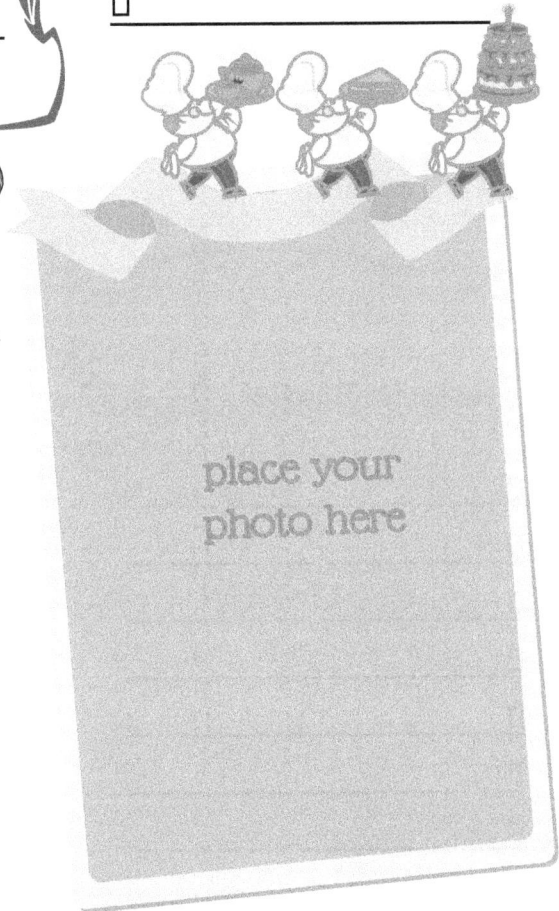
place your
photo here

Travel Journal

Date _____

_____
Place to Explore

i ♥ NYC

Things to See & Do :

- [ ] ....
- [ ] ....
- [ ] ....
- [ ] ....
- [ ] ....
- [ ] ....
- [ ] ....
- [ ] ....
- [ ] ....
- [ ] ....

Things to Observe :

- [ ] _____
- [ ] _____
- [ ] _____
- [ ] _____
- [ ] _____
- [ ] _____
- [ ] _____

Places to Mingle :

- [ ] _____
- [ ] _____
- [ ] _____
- [ ] _____
- [ ] _____
- [ ] _____
- [ ] _____

Adventure to Have :

- [ ] _____
- [ ] _____
- [ ] _____
- [ ] _____
- [ ] _____
- [ ] _____
- [ ] _____

Travel Journal

i ♥ NYC

Sreets to Check Out :

☐ _____

☐ _____

☐ _____

☐ _____

☐ _____

☐ _____

☐ _____

People to Meet :

☐ _____

☐ _____

☐ _____

☐ _____

☐ _____

☐ _____

☐ _____

Shops to Visit :

☐ _____

☐ _____

☐ _____

☐ _____

☐ _____

☐ _____

☐ _____

place your photo here

Travel Journal

i ♥ NYC

Date _____   _____
                     Place to Explore

Things to See & Do :

- ☐ ....
- ☐ ....
- ☐ ....
- ☐ ....
- ☐ ....
- ☐ ....
- ☐ ....
- ☐ ....
- ☐ ....
- ☐ ....

Things to Observe :

- ☐ _____
- ☐ _____
- ☐ _____
- ☐ _____
- ☐ _____
- ☐ _____
- ☐ _____

Places to Mingle : 🍴♡🍴

- ☐ _____
- ☐ _____
- ☐ _____
- ☐ _____
- ☐ _____
- ☐ _____
- ☐ _____

Adventure to Have :

- ☐ _____
- ☐ _____
- ☐ _____
- ☐ _____
- ☐ _____
- ☐ _____

Travel Journal

i ♥ NYC

Sreets to Check Out :

- ☐ _____
- ☐ _____
- ☐ _____
- ☐ _____
- ☐ _____
- ☐ _____
- ☐ _____

People to Meet :

- ☐ _____
- ☐ _____
- ☐ _____
- ☐ _____
- ☐ _____
- ☐ _____
- ☐ _____

Shops to Visit :

- ☐ _____
- ☐ _____
- ☐ _____
- ☐ _____
- ☐ _____
- ☐ _____
- ☐ _____

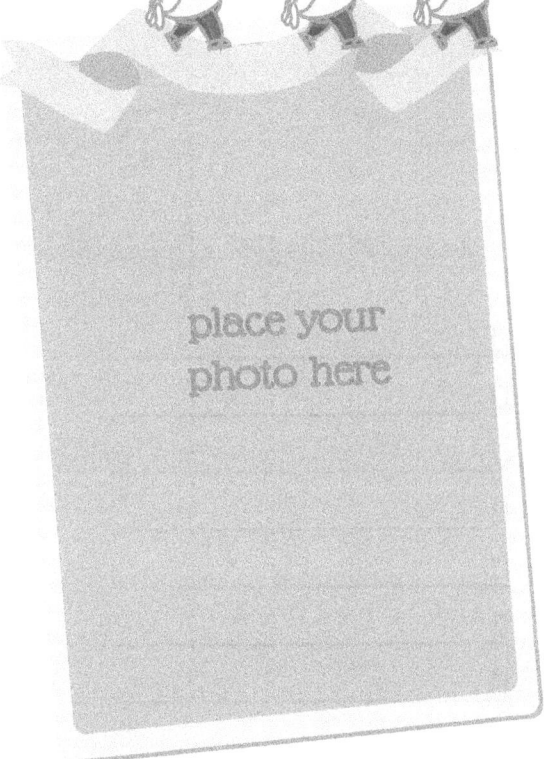
place your photo here

Travel Journal

Date _____

_____
Place to Explore

i ♥ NYC

Things to See & Do :

- ☐ ....
- ☐ ....
- ☐ ....
- ☐ ....
- ☐ ....
- ☐ ....
- ☐ ....
- ☐ ....
- ☐ ....

Things to Observe :

- ☐ _____
- ☐ _____
- ☐ _____
- ☐ _____
- ☐ _____
- ☐ _____
- ☐ _____

Places to Mingle :

- ☐ _____
- ☐ _____
- ☐ _____
- ☐ _____
- ☐ _____
- ☐ _____
- ☐ _____

Adventure to Have :

- ☐ _____
- ☐ _____
- ☐ _____
- ☐ _____
- ☐ _____
- ☐ _____
- ☐ _____

Travel Journal

i ♥ NYC

Sreets to Check Out :

- ☐ _____
- ☐ _____
- ☐ _____
- ☐ _____
- ☐ _____
- ☐ _____
- ☐ _____

People to Meet :

- ☐ _____
- ☐ _____
- ☐ _____
- ☐ _____
- ☐ _____
- ☐ _____
- ☐ _____

Shops to Visit :

- ☐ _____
- ☐ _____
- ☐ _____
- ☐ _____
- ☐ _____
- ☐ _____
- ☐ _____

place your
photo here

Travel Journal

i ♥ NYC

Date _____

_____
Place to Explore

Things to See & Do :

☐ ....
☐ ....
☐ ....
☐ ....
☐ ....
☐ ....
☐ ....
☐ ....
☐ ....
☐ ....

Things to Observe :

☐ _____
☐ _____
☐ _____
☐ _____
☐ _____
☐ _____
☐ _____

Places to Mingle :

☐ _____
☐ _____
☐ _____
☐ _____
☐ _____
☐ _____
☐ _____

Adventure to Have :

☐ _____
☐ _____
☐ _____
☐ _____
☐ _____
☐ _____
☐ _____

Travel Journal

i ♥ NYC

Sreets to Check Out :

☐ _____
☐ _____
☐ _____
☐ _____
☐ _____
☐ _____
☐ _____

People to Meet :

☐ _____
☐ _____
☐ _____
☐ _____
☐ _____
☐ _____
☐ _____

Shops to Visit :

☐ _____
☐ _____
☐ _____
☐ _____
☐ _____
☐ _____
☐ _____

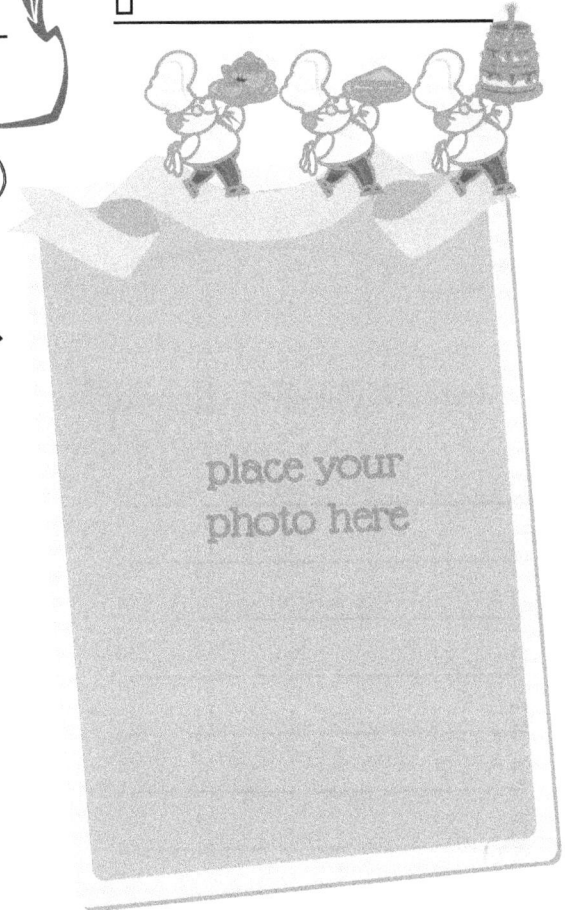

place your
photo here

Travel Journal

Date _____

_____
Place to Explore

i
♥
NYC

Things to See & Do :

- ☐ ....
- ☐ ....
- ☐ ....
- ☐ ....
- ☐ ....
- ☐ ....
- ☐ ....
- ☐ ....
- ☐ ....
- ☐ ....

Things to Observe :

- ☐ _____
- ☐ _____
- ☐ _____
- ☐ _____
- ☐ _____
- ☐ _____
- ☐ _____

Places to Mingle :

- ☐ _____
- ☐ _____
- ☐ _____
- ☐ _____
- ☐ _____
- ☐ _____
- ☐ _____

Adventure to Have :

- ☐ _____
- ☐ _____
- ☐ _____
- ☐ _____
- ☐ _____
- ☐ _____
- ☐ _____

Travel Journal

i ♥ NYC

Sreets to Check Out :

- ☐ _____
- ☐ _____
- ☐ _____
- ☐ _____
- ☐ _____
- ☐ _____
- ☐ _____

People to Meet :

- ☐ _____
- ☐ _____
- ☐ _____
- ☐ _____
- ☐ _____
- ☐ _____
- ☐ _____

Shops to Visit :

- ☐ _____
- ☐ _____
- ☐ _____
- ☐ _____
- ☐ _____
- ☐ _____
- ☐ _____

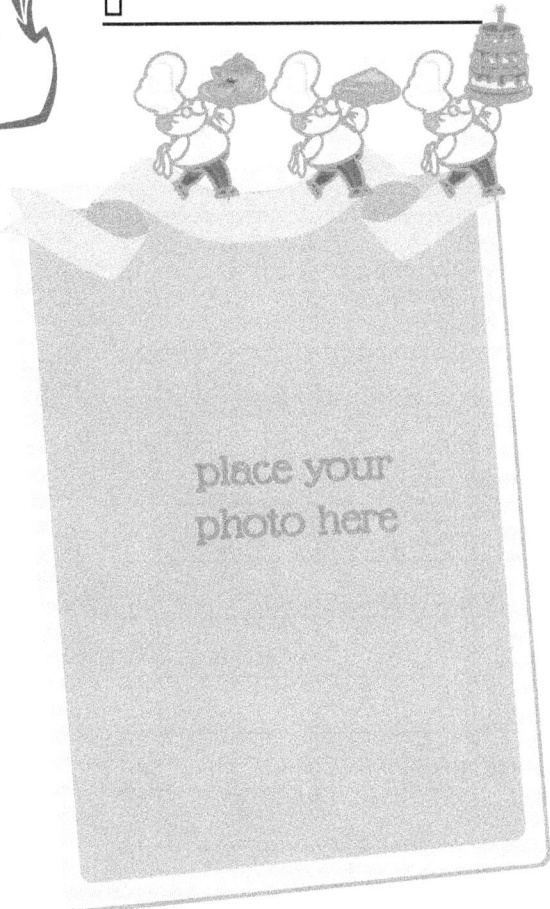

place your photo here

Travel Journal

i ♥ NYC

Date _____

_____
Place to Explore

Things to See & Do :

☐ ....
☐ ....
☐ ....
☐ ....
☐ ....
☐ ....
☐ ....
☐ ....
☐ ....
☐ ....

Things to Observe :

☐ _____
☐ _____
☐ _____
☐ _____
☐ _____
☐ _____
☐ _____

Places to Mingle :

☐ _____
☐ _____
☐ _____
☐ _____
☐ _____
☐ _____
☐ _____

Adventure to Have :

☐ _____
☐ _____
☐ _____
☐ _____
☐ _____
☐ _____
☐ _____

Travel Journal

i ❤ NYC

Sreets to Check Out :

- ☐ _____
- ☐ _____
- ☐ _____
- ☐ _____
- ☐ _____
- ☐ _____
- ☐ _____

People to Meet :

- ☐ _____
- ☐ _____
- ☐ _____
- ☐ _____
- ☐ _____
- ☐ _____
- ☐ _____

Shops to Visit :

- ☐ _____
- ☐ _____
- ☐ _____
- ☐ _____
- ☐ _____
- ☐ _____
- ☐ _____

place your
photo here